MERCHANTS OF WINE

MERCHANTS OF WINE

Being a Centenary Account of the Fortunes of the House of Gilbey

by
ALEC WAUGH

With a frontispiece and sixteen pages of half-tone illustrations

CASSELL AND COMPANY LTD
LONDON

CASSELL & CO. LTD
37/38 ST. ANDREW'S HILL
QUEEN VICTORIA STREET
LONDON, E.C.4

and at

31/34 GEORGE IV BRIDGE, EDINBURGH
210 QUEEN STREET, MELBOURNE
26/30 CLARENCE STREET, SYDNEY
24 WYNDHAM STREET, AUCKLAND, NEW ZEALAND
1068 BROADVIEW AVENUE, TORONTO 6
P.O. BOX 275, CAPE TOWN
P.O. BOX 11190, JOHANNESBURG
P.O. BOX 189, BRIDGETOWN, BARBADOS
HAROON CHAMBERS, SOUTH NAPIER ROAD, KARACHI
13/14 AJMERI GATE EXTENSION, NEW DELHI 1
15 GRAHAM ROAD, BALLARD ESTATE, BOMBAY 1
17 CHITTARANJAN AVENUE, CALCUTTA 13
MACDONALD HOUSE, ORCHARD ROAD, SINGAPORE 9
P.O. BOX 959, ACCRA, GOLD COAST
AVENIDA 9 DE JULHO 1138, SÃO PAULO
GALERIA GÜEMES, ESCRITORIO 454/59 FLORIDA 165, BUENOS AIRES
MARNE 5B, MEXICO 5, D.F.
25 RUE HENRI BARBUSSE, PARIS 5E
25 NY STRANDVEJ, ESPERGAERDE, DENMARK
KAUWLAAN 17, THE HAGUE

First published 1957

Set in Bell type and made and printed in Great Britain by William Clowes and Sons, Limited, London and Beccles
F.1156

Contents

List of Illustrations

List of Illustrations

With drawings by Robin Jacques

CHAPTER I

How It All Began

IN March 1856 the last shots of the Crimean War were exchanged, and the campaign fizzled out, in a bitterly cold Black Sea spring, with race meetings for officers, and ceremonial, inter-allied reviews of grumbling guardsmen, zouaves, bersaglieri and bashibazouks.

At home in England, people turned with a sigh of relief from casualty lists, reports of military mismanagement, and votes of censure, to chatter excitedly about the burning down of Covent Garden Opera House and to read, horribly fascinated, the macabre accounts of Dr. Palmer's experiments with strychnine at Rugeley. In Paris the beautiful Eugénie was brought to bed of a boy destined to fall in a foreign cause on a battlefield even further away from France than the Crimea.

For many English people—for the great majority, indeed—the end of the muddled and grossly mismanaged war came as a relief. But the end of a war comes always as a problem to many a young man: what do I do now? And so it was with, among many others, two young men—brothers—for whom the end of the war meant, or might well mean, the beginning of a search for a livelihood.

Walter and Alfred Gilbey were civilian clerks, who for two years had been bent over their desks in the Army Pay Department at the base at Gallipoli; and the end of the war left them where they had been at its beginning. They had started with nothing, and they had nothing to go back to. They had their way to make without inherited capital or savings. But they had one thing which they might very properly value much more highly—a name that they could honour.

The Gilbeys came of sound Essex stock. Their great-grandfather had been the forester on the great Hallingbury estate; their grandfather, Daniel Gilbey, born in 1759, had owned three public houses at Stansted, 'The White Bear', 'The Bell' and 'The Rose and Crown'; their father, Henry, had been a coach-proprietor on the London–Bishop's Stortford run. For a brief period he had been relatively prosperous. The skill of Macadam had in the early years of the nineteenth century transformed the English highways from a labyrinth of ruts into a smooth hard surface. The mail service was fast and punctual, maintaining an average speed of ten miles an hour. On the Great North Road, one for every mile between Edinburgh and London, stood four hundred horses. Henry Gilbey did the thirty miles return trip to London daily. It was a section of the direct route to Cambridge and Newmarket, and it brought him into contact with a variety of different types. His reputation stood high among them. Jovial and a good raconteur, he was popular with the passengers; the Prince Regent had, indeed, once given him a horse. The future had seemed so assured that he had complete confidence in his ability to provide sustenance and education for six sons and as many daughters.

It often happens, however, that no sooner has a certain method been perfected than it becomes obsolete. In 1789, the year of Henry Gilbey's birth, Erasmus Darwin had included in his *Loves of the Plants* the unpoetic but prophetic couplet:

> Soon shall thine arm, resistless steam, afar
> Drag the slow barge and drive the rapid car.

Scarcely one of his readers imagined that swifter means of

communication could be invented than horses by land and sails by sea. Yet in the same way that the clipper ships were to be displaced by steamers, the mail coach, during the eighteen-thirties, was to be discarded in favour of the steam locomotive, and Henry Gilbey, like Sam Weller's father, was a ruined man.

He died in 1842, leaving his three surviving sons nothing except his name, and possibly his example. Conservative by nature, he had refused to believe in new inventions. There could be no competition, he insisted, in a rival that 'wouldn't even stop to pick up passengers'. Possibly his sons profited by his example. For if the success of the House of Gilbey can be attributed to any one characteristic it is to an instinctive ability to anticipate change and adapt its policy and programme to it.

When the Crimean campaign ended, Walter Gilbey was twenty-six years old and Alfred twenty-four. They found themselves on their return not only with no occupation and no capital, but with no obvious assets to place upon the market; they had no special training. They had however energy, enterprise and a capacity for work. And that was all that was needed of a young Englishman in the middle of the nineteenth century. The most prolonged boom in English history was under way. Europe, exhausted with wars and revolutions, was desperately in need of manufactured articles: where was she to look for them? The New World? For the American frontier had spread to the Pacific. Vast territories were becoming states; raw materials were flowing to the factories; it might well have been that the United States would have done much to satisfy the demands of the Old World for consumer goods, had it not been that the country was spending too much of its pioneering energy on getting rich quick in the gold mines of California, in land-grabbing in the southwest, and that the tension already existed that was to snap into a civil war.

Britain, on the other hand, with an empire that was both consolidated and expanding; with India's princes about to recognize Victoria as their Empress; Britain, undistracted by conflict, external or internal, stood at the centre of the world; her ships its carriers; her looms and lathes ready for its raw materials; her bankers, experienced, astute, reliable, equipped to organize its trade. Tariff barriers were down and Navigation Acts repealed. Agriculture had not yet been undermined through the import of cheap American wheat. Coal in abundance could purchase raw materials. Europe, in industrial machinery, was a generation behind her. Great fortunes were to be made by Englishmen during the next half-century. There was a vast field for enterprise and energy to till, and the two young Gilbeys were not the men to leave the ploughshares rusting.

Before the war, Walter had been employed, in a very humble capacity, in a firm of Parliamentary agents. It was clear that no particularly bright or lucrative future lay in that direction. Alfred, however, had worked in a wine business, of which their eldest brother was one of the proprietors, and here, surely, was a key to success.

This brother, Henry Parry Gilbey, had been born in 1824 and educated at Christ's Hospital, to which he was presented by Christopher Smith, M.P., a wine merchant, and Lord Mayor of London in 1817.* Christopher Smith's partner was James Church Bailey, uncle to young Henry, who, when he left school, was taken into the office of Smith, Bailey & Co., thus forging the first link in the long chain connecting the Gilbey family with the wine trade.

In 1842 the partnership of Smith, Bailey & Co. was dissolved, and new businesses were formed under the names of Smith & Co., and James Church Bailey & Co. Henry Parry Gilbey went into the office of his uncle and remained with him until, in 1851, he joined in establishing the firm of Southard, Gilbey & Co. as wholesale wine merchants in the City of London.

It was natural that the wine trade should have promised the likeliest opening to the two young Gilbeys and, on Henry Parry's advice, they decided to start a business as retail wine merchants. Taking cellars at the corner of Berwick Street and Oxford Street, they set up the sign over its front door, 'W. & A. Gilbey', in February 1857, less than a year after the end of the Crimean War.

* Christopher Smith's business was founded in 1784, and continues to the present time in Oporto under the name of Smith, Woodhouse & Co., one of the oldest and most highly respected firms in the wine trade.

H. G. Wells once said that 'timeliness' was the most essential ingredient in the make-up of a best-selling novelist. The same characteristic is required in a merchant; he needs the capacity to turn the caprice and chances of the hour to his advantage; and though they could not have foreseen it, the young Gilbeys put up their sign not only at a propitious but at a dramatic moment.

The wine trade in England has known many fluctuations (which may be studied at length in the writings of that fine scholar and historian, André Simon). The cold and clammy chill of its long winters has always made wines and spirits, if not essential ingredients, at any rate highly desirable concomitants of the English diet. Historians have presumed that wine, and perhaps even the vine, was imported by the Romans; certainly in the ninth century regular shipments were being made from Rouen; while in the middle of the twelfth century the marriage of Henry Plantagenet and Eleanor of Aquitaine placed the vineyards of the Gironde under the English Crown. The popularity of Gascon wines was indeed responsible for the birth of the English Navy, for when, in the second quarter of the fourteenth century, Edward III's currency restrictions forced the Bordeaux merchants to establish their bases across the Channel, the English had to build a fleet to fetch their wine.

Edward III's reign is also noticeable in the history of wine for the forging of the first links with Portugal; a treaty had been arranged which allowed Portuguese ships to fish for cod off the English coasts and, during the days on shore, wine brought over in skins and casks was bartered for English manufactured goods. This trade was to have a further influence on the spread in England of a taste for Portuguese wine; for, after the Reformation, when the country gradually ceased to observe the Lenten fast and Ember Days, the Devonshire and Cornish sailors could find no home sale for the dried Newfoundland cod that had been the staple fish days' diet. They had to seek markets overseas, and Portugal, a Catholic country, was ready to accept 'penitential cod' in return for wine.

It was not, however, the port we know that the merchants of this period brought back in exchange for fish, but a table wine not from the Douro district but from Minho, some fifty miles further north.

Tastes in wine change and, by the time that the founder of Eton College had lost England her French possessions, English taste was turning away from claret towards the sweet wines of Spain, Portugal and Italy. After the loss of Aquitaine, the chief French import was a thin vintage from Poitou shipped from La Rochelle. There was a vogue for Cypriot Malmsey; sack from Spain was introduced in the sixteenth century, and the close of the seventeenth century saw the introduction of port.

In 1678, so we are assured by that sound historian F. A. Cockburn, two young sons of an English wine merchant who had been sent to Portugal to learn the business were entertained at a local monastery outside Oporto with a wine that so delighted them that they shipped back to their father as much of it as they could buy, having fortified it first with brandy. Its popularity in England was instantaneous, and André Simon used the poem *Search of Claret* published in 1691, with its references to red and white port being sold in London taverns by the glass or bottle, as proof of his contention that subsequent legislation continued and confirmed a taste rather than created it. So strong had become the preference for cordials and spirits, that by the end of the seventeenth century, when William III raised the duties on wine, the import of French beverages had practically ceased. The final nail was struck home into the coffin by the Methuen Treaty of 1703 which, with the express intention of destroying the French wine trade, admitted Portuguese wines, in return for certain concessions with regard to English woollens, at a duty of £7 a tun, whereas French wines had to pay £55. Port so set the fashion through the eighteenth century that at the start of the nineteenth it was held that the first duty of a wine was to be red, then sweet.

In the middle of the nineteenth century, therefore, when Henry Parry Gilbey was entering the wine trade, the general taste was for dark vintage ports, full sweet sherries and madeiras. Wealthier people drank sweet champagne, and only the well-to-do with a cultivated palate drank burgundy and claret. There was a duty on French wine of twelve shillings a case, and the maximum import in the best years was well under a quarter of a million gallons.

There was, however, a growing market for colonial wines, and particularly for South African. Upon Cape wines, as they were called, the duty was half that which was levied upon French imports, and Henry Parry advised his brothers to concentrate upon this branch of the trade, recommending them to aim at acquiring a reputation for the supply of clean, wholesome, cheap wines at a small rate of profit; if, he argued, they once acquired that reputation, they could rely on a steady middle-class clientèle. And their first step was to insert in the *Morning Advertiser* of February 23, 1857, a half-inch advertisement offering Cape port and sherry at 20*s*. a dozen, and brandy at 30*s*. a dozen, two samples for twelve stamps.

Throughout that autumn, similar advertisements in *The Times*, headed 'Wines from the Cape of Good Hope', explained the prices with the phrase, 'Produce of Spanish and Portuguese vines at the Cape of Good Hope, whence Her Majesty's Government allow wines to be imported for half duty.' And the little firm was only some eight months old when a rather patronizing reference, in a *Times* leader, to the fact that the Cape and other countries 'may be capable of producing excellent grapes and excellent wine', but that claret and burgundy had possession of the market, and that 'if we went any further it is by no means unlikely that we should fare rather worse', set either Walter or Alfred to his writing-desk the day after its appearance in print, and on October 15, 1857, appeared the letter:

Wines from the Cape of Good Hope

In one of your leading articles of yesterday, you say that it is asserted that the Cape of Good Hope is capable of producing excellent wine. We are in a condition not only to substantiate that assertion but have, during the past few months that we have made use of your columns, convinced an unprecedented number of good judges that the wines of the Cape of Good Hope are equal in quality to most of the produce of the Continent and decidedly superior to the second qualities of Portugal and Spain.

While the success of introducing these wines has exceeded expectations, our colonists at the Cape have publicly expressed their appreciation of their cause being advocated in your journal which has assisted in increasing the value of their wines in this market nearly double, and enabled them to ship this year four times a larger quantity than usual.

We are, Sir, your most obedient servants,
W. & A. GILBEY.

October 13*th*, 1857.

So popular, indeed, did these Cape wines prove that within a few months Walter's and Alfred's firm had 20,000 customers on its books; by the end of its second year the premises in Berwick Street had grown too small, and a new office was opened at 357 Oxford Street. Moreover, so many orders were coming in from Ireland that a branch establishment had to be established in Dublin, and plans were under discussion for the opening of further branches in Edinburgh and Belfast. These plans were shortly implemented.

In a period such as ours it may well seem astonishing that a new two-man firm could make so swift a start. But in 1857 private enterprise was unfettered by controls; there were no forms to be filled up, no waiting in queues in draughty corridors to placate officials. Because of the vast cost of the war, income tax had risen to the giddy and unprecedented height of one-and-fourpence in the pound, but it came down almost immediately to the more normal sevenpence, which meant that profits could be ploughed back. The financing of the firm supplied few problems. When Walter Gilbey was asked in later days with what capital the firm had started he replied 'the proverbial half-crown'. Its only capital, indeed, was the good standing in the city of Henry Parry Gilbey, but that was enough for the obtaining of adequate facilities, and the business was largely financed by accommodation bills.

Those were still curiously primitive days of banking. Purchases of wine on the Continent were paid for by short-dated bills of three, six or nine months' date. These bills were frequently passed from hand to hand like bank notes, and often came back with additional paper gummed to the back to take all the endorsements of the various firms through which they had passed. How many of the plots of Victorian novels depend upon the hero's having 'backed a bill' that the villain cannot meet? These mysterious 'bills' are commoner in Trollope, say, than dud cheques in the novels of our own time. Payment by cheque was not, in fact, a general practice, and customers frequently settled their accounts by cutting bank notes in half and sending each half by a different post, so that a clerk had to be employed in sticking the two halves together on receipt. Men who had the capacity for making money made it fast in those days, and Walter and Alfred had that capacity in full measure.

SIR WALTER GILBEY, Baronet

1831–1914

From the Painting by W. Q. Orchardson, R.A., which was presented to Sir Walter Gilbey together with a Painting of Lady Gilbey by the same Artist, in the name of 1234 subscribers by His Majesty King Edward VII (then H.R.H. The Prince of Wales) on March 3rd, 1891

Gilbey's Four-in-Hand and Coach. Painting by Lionel Edwards, R.I.

Gilbey's One-horse van. Scene from film *The Barretts of Wimpole Street*

Gilbey's Coach at Richmond Horse Show

Gilbey's Two-horse delivery turnout

The Pantheon, Oxford Street, in the Regency Period

A Masquerade in the Pantheon

Gilbey's General Office in the Pantheon—1907

The Round House, Camden Town

Other members of the family had it too. Two of Walter's sisters had become engaged to two brothers, Henry and Charles Gold, who were promptly enrolled in the new enterprise. Between the Golds and Gilbeys there was a certain kinship of situation, each family having been the victim of a reverse of fortune. The Golds' grandfather, a prosperous Birmingham manufacturer, having been struck by lightning—of all melodramatic misfortunes to befall a Midland ironmonger!—was defrauded by his partner while he was still weak from his mishap and away from business. He chivalrously refrained from prosecuting, since the punishment at the time was transportation for life, but he lost all his capital, and the young Golds, like the young Gilbeys, were launched without resources upon the world of work.

Henry Gold joined the firm at its very start, and his order book, still in existence, shows that he was first employed as a salesman. Before joining his brothers-in-law he had been apprenticed to a law stationer, and his exquisite handwriting can no doubt be attributed to his training there. He proved his worth sufficiently in his new capacity to be entrusted with the management of the Dublin branch, while a year later his brother Charles opened the Scottish branch in Edinburgh.

There were other newcomers in Henry Arthur Blyth and James Blyth, nephews of the Gilbeys, the sons of their eldest sister. Henry Arthur Blyth, the younger, entered at the age of fourteen straight from school. His strong point was figures and eventually he was given charge of the finances. By insisting on the prompt and regular settlement of accounts, he helped to establish the firm's credit with the trade.* James—his elder by two years—had some experience in the wine trade, having been employed by a firm that also specialized in Cape wines, but as he was only seventeen when he joined his uncles the experience was as near as possible to being negligible.

* The quarterly balance was a regular feature of the firm and in the early days the results of the quarter's trading were on the Board table on the morning of the first day of the new quarter. This meant working most of the night. The partners all lived near the Pantheon and would come back again after dinner to help write the figures. The Chief Accountant, A. G. Carver, lived at Shepherds Bush and had to walk back there at 3 a.m.

One other surname was to be added, that of Grinling; Henry Grinling, the son of Henry Gilbey's sister-in-law—who had been with Walter and Alfred in the Crimea—resigning in 1865 his appointment at the War Office to join the firm; in the following year he became a partner.

Those three surnames—Gold, Blyth and Grinling—are the only ones, apart from Gilbey, that have figured on the list of partners in the hundred years' history of the firm. The House of Gilbey has always been a family firm; that is its strength as it is its personality. With the exception of Antony Grinling and his son Jasper, the grandson and great-grandson respectively of Henry Grinling, who was a cousin by marriage of the original partners, every director of the company today is a great- or great-great-grandson of the original Henry Gilbey who 'took the ribbons' on the Cambridge road.

CHAPTER II

Gladstone's Budget

AT the southern end of Camden High Street, in the islanded centre of the busy junction by Mornington Crescent Underground Station, stands a typically Victorian statue of a typically Victorian figure. The chalky grey stone has weathered badly—in less than ninety years the monitory right hand of the frock-coated statesman has been worn by wind and rain and the erosion of London's grime into a pathetic stump, but clearly discernible on the plinth—to anybody interested enough in a remarkably unattractive memorial to brave the whirlpool of cars and trolley-buses and reach the little island site—is the inscription:

ERECTED
BY
PUBLIC SUBSCRIPTION
TO WHICH
NAPOLEON III
WAS PRINCIPAL CONTRIBUTOR

COBDEN

PRESENTED
TO THE
VESTRY OF ST. PANCRAS
JUNE 1868

The statue is not more than half a mile from Gilbey House, and it is to be hoped that directors of the firm today, passing it, spare Richard Cobden and Napoleon III a kindly thought apiece, and perhaps even a friendly salute. But in 1868, when it was presented to the Vestry of St. Pancras, the partners of the time might have been forgiven for a less polite gesture. It would have been short-sighted, as history has turned out, but in the eighteen-sixties it would have been understandable.

For if fortunes were made quickly in the eighteen-sixties, reverses could come upon an infant enterprise with equal suddenness. Within two years of their opening, the future of W. and A. Gilbey had seemed assured. The premises in Oxford Street had proved, happily, to be as inadequate as those in Berwick Street, and new and bigger ones still had been acquired in Great Titchfield Street—premises that extended at the rear into buildings in Wells Street. Two branch establishments had been opened, and so big was the trade in Cape wines that it was felt necessary for the firm to have a representative on the spot, to superintend the shipping. James Blyth was given the job, but before he could sail, even, an event took place that was to change completely the drinking habits of the nation—and of Gilbey's customers.

Although the two countries had been allies so recently in the Crimea, feeling ran high between France and Britain in 1859: Professor G. M. Trevelyan is certain that we not only came near to war, but that if Palmerston had been as firmly in the Parliamentary saddle as he had been a couple of years earlier, war would probably have broken out.

In the autumn of that year, 1859, Gladstone, the Chancellor of the Exchequer, and Cobden, the Radical Member for Rochdale, strolled through the fallen leaves in the garden at Hawarden, Gladstone's house in the country. How was peace to be preserved when a carbon-copy Napoleon was rattling the sabre in France, and in England the Poet Laureate was trumpeting to his fellow-countrymen:

'Form, form, Riflemen, form!'

The answer was that England, as Napoleon's own uncle had

once observed, was a nation of shopkeepers. What Cobden proposed, that September day at Hawarden, was a commercial treaty with France, 'the free-trade advantages of which', as Professor Trevelyan has observed, 'bore down the clamour for war in our island.' Cobden himself went over to Paris and talked Napoleon, in person, into a commercial treaty that gave France 'most-favoured nation' treatment and brought down immediately the duty on French wines to no more than the duty on any other.

The provisions of the treaty were embodied in Gladstone's budget of 1860: the duty on French table wines tumbled from twelve shillings to two shillings a dozen; and the Cape wine trade received a blow from which it did not recover for nearly three-quarters of a century.

To a firm as young as the Gilbeys' this unexpected turn of events threatened to prove as catastrophic as had the introduction of the steam locomotive to the mail coach. The business had been based upon Cape wines, and clearly such wines could no longer enter into competition with French wines that paid the same duty. They had, however, profited by the example of old Henry Gilbey. They had learnt, in a hard school, that one must accept and adapt oneself to new conditions. They did not sit back and say 'Disraeli will restore Empire preference.' Seeing nothing but ruin for the particular kind of business they had built up, they decided to risk everything on a hazardous experiment by following in a new field Henry Parry Gilbey's original advice to supply the British public with cheap, clean, wholesome wine; and they applied his principles by treating claret from Bordeaux in the same way that they had treated dessert wines from the Cape.

They were alone in doing this. The trade in general had no faith in what it called 'Gladstone claret'. It considered French wine a luxury for the rich, and refused to share the Chancellor of the Exchequer's expectation that the cheaper Médoc wines would supplant the national taste for Cape wines. The old-established firms made no effort to reduce the price of claret and burgundy in any proper relation to the reduction in duty. That was the Gilbeys' chance, and they took it promptly, promising to allow their customers the full benefit that accrued from the lowering of the duty. They handled wine as any businessman handles any other commercial article, offering it on the open market at a price proportionate to the cost of its production. In the *Morning Advertiser* of 1860 they were announcing Bordeaux wines at 18*s.* a dozen.

In every career there is a point of crisis when a short cut must be taken, a bold decision made if an escape out of the rut is to be effected. If the opportunity, when it comes, is missed, it may have gone for ever. The postman does not always knock twice. This was the moment for the Gilbeys. If they had hesitated, if they had followed the example of the trade—a course of action that was followed with some success by firms who had a loyal and assured clientèle—and, while switching from Cape to French wines, had kept for themselves the major part of the profit arising from the reduced duty, they would certainly, because of their energy, youth and enterprise, have retained many of their old customers, and perhaps even acquired new ones. It is impossible to believe that such industrious, competent and energetic young men as the Gilbeys and the Golds, the Blyths and Henry Grinling would not in any circumstances have proved reasonably successful in any enterprise they undertook. But if they had missed this opportunity, they would in all human probability have remained cosily obscure. As it was, by that one short cut they set themselves apart, unrivalled and unchallenged: they had a clear lead; they were out in the open, the field to themselves.

They won then a position which they have never lost. As the late Sir Herbert Maxwell wrote on the fiftieth anniversary of the house, 'The rope which at first seemed about to drag the firm to inevitable dissolution proved in effect the mainstay of its fortunes.' Figures soon proved the extent to which the trade was wrong in the belief that nobody would drink 'Gladstone claret'. Before the budget of 1860 the yearly import in the best years failed to touch a quarter of a million gallons; in 1868, by the time Richard Cobden's statue was being put up in Camden High Street, four and a half millions were imported.

The extent to which Gladstone's budget altered the drinking habits of the English can be judged by comparing the kind of hospitality offered by Dickens's characters in the middle of the century with that offered at the close of the century in George and Weedon Grossmiths' *The Diary of a Nobody*. There is not a great deal of wine drunk by Dickens's characters. They are for beer and grogs, punches and mulled brews, though it was, admittedly, 'old port—claret—good—very good', at the cricket dinner at Dingley Dell, according to Mr. Jingle, that made Mr. Snodgrass look so poorly. '"It wasn't the wine," murmured Mr. Snodgrass in a broken voice, "it was the salmon."' And it was on brandy and water that Mr. Jorrocks and James Pigg made the classic discovery that the night was hellish dark and smelled of cheese.

Mr. Pooter, on the other hand, the Grossmiths' 'Nobody', a suburban member of the less affluent white-collar class, half a century later invariably entertains his guests with champagne. Port and sherry are on his sideboard. The champagne that he acquires from his grocer is not of a well-known brand, it is labelled *Jackson Frères*, it is non-vintage but it costs only 3*s*. 6*d*. a bottle. Sherry, 'dry and nut', is 1*s*. 3*d*. Whisky is offered at 2*s*. 6*d*. with twopence back on the bottle. But it is only because he has a cold that he orders whisky. There is no reference to gin. True, Mr. Pooter is a caricature, a figure of fun, but it was due to the genius of the Grossmiths that he was recognizably close to real life: such a figure *could* exist; he *could* buy champagne from his grocer; and it *would* be about three-and-sixpence a bottle.

It was not only by the new price of claret that the Budget of 1860 gave an opening to the foresight, enterprise and acumen of a rising firm. A further clause in it was to have an equally marked effect on the Gilbeys' fortunes. Before 1860 the retailing of wine to the individual customer had been restricted by law to hotel-keepers, publicans and wine merchants. But Gladstone realized that the individual customer of moderate means now needed to make from a nearby shop individual purchases of single bottles of wine and spirits which he could take home. Gladstone, product though he was of Eton and the House, had made himself, by his Budget of 1860, the radical leader of the lower middle classes: it was part of his political genius to recognize the needs of Mr. Pooter.

Gladstone's 'single bottle' Act of 1861, by the institution of 'off-licences', threw the wine trade open. Previously a dealer had to pay ten guineas for a licence; but now any grocer could sell wine to be consumed off the premises in quart or pint bottles. The Act also allowed 'keepers of refreshment houses of good repute to sell wine on the premises'. It was a change of which the Gilbeys were quick to recognize the advantage for themselves. They no longer needed to deal with their consuming customers direct; from their headquarters in London and their branches in Edinburgh and Dublin, they could now operate through a series of agents owning such off-licences. Relieved of the expense of canvassers and travellers, of endless petty book-keeping, of the time involved in dealing with individual customers, they could concentrate on the quality of the wines supplied and on the advertising of their wares. Their business could be limited to finding the right kind of agent, giving him the monopoly in his allotted district, then seeing that he was satisfied and that he satisfied his customers.

Reading, Torquay and Wolverhampton were the first towns in which agents were appointed, but soon from all parts of the country applications for appointment were pouring in. It is said that many of these first agents were country stationmasters, because of their unparalleled opportunities both for handling and storing cases and for recognizing and exploiting local custom. If that was so, then the wheel, in a way, had come full circle, for the railway companies that had ruined Henry Gilbey, the coachman, were now contributing to the prosperity of his sons. Later, the companies disallowed the practice, but by then the agency principle was established. In a few years the great majority of customers drew their supplies through local agencies instead of from the Oxford Street headquarters.

Within less than ten years of setting up their first sign in Berwick Street, the partners had made the label 'Gilbey' a familiar and honoured trademark throughout the country.

CHAPTER III

How the Business Spread

EVERY success story, whether of a man or of a firm, will be found to follow a pattern, and in most cases one of two patterns. It is either a man pitted against his day, or a man aided by his day—a man swimming with or against the tide, in other words—with the man's personality worked upon either by the particular difficulties or by the particular opportunities that his day presents. As with individual men, so too with business houses, there are equally two main divisions of success stories. There is the success that comes at the end of a long struggle after many reverses, and there is the success that comes from the consolidation and development of an early triumphant venture. The first type is the more obviously dramatic, but the second type demands just as much skill, courage and resolution and, it may well be, greater subtlety and intelligence. The victor who has earned his first laurels easily is faced with two temptations: he either becomes over-confident, too ready to believe that any gamble will come off, that everything he touches will turn to gold, or he becomes lazy and complacent, all too ready to rest on his achievement. It takes solid character and hard work, as many war-lords have discovered, to exploit steadily over the years the potentialities of an early victory.

The Gilbeys' story is of the second kind, as are so many histories of the growth of family businesses in England throughout the Victorian age. Which is the reason why, perhaps, as a recent essayist in the *Economist* has pointed out:

> At a time when the British business man was conquering the world, Victorian novelists saw little of interest in him. *John Halifax, Gentleman* (the title is significant) is a full-length study; but one has to search Meredith, George Eliot, or even Disraeli to find a substantial business man. Here and there in Thackeray or Trollope a business man—usually a merchant—is seen struggling to rise in genteel society. Aristocrats and farmers; the learned professions and the artists; soldiers, seamen, politicians, schoolmasters—all appear in the gallery of Victorian portraiture, their background often rendered with a fine knowledge of the technicalities involved. But the factory, even the bank or export house, hardly appear at all.

Be the reason what it may, it is true that the story of Gilbey's is not a dramatic record of ups and downs. There have been no crises, no dark moments of suspense. Danger had not flashed its bright eyes at the young enterprise. But all this was only because the founders moved always with forethought and with foresight, never deserting the principles on which their firm was built. They recognized that their problem was different from that of other wine merchants. They were not dealing with private customers whose personal idiosyncrasies had to be cajoled and cherished; they were operating through a series of agencies, and their wares had to be standardized so that a Gilbey claret bought at Reading, say, should have the same look and taste as a claret bought in Wolverhampton—that a consumer, in other words, could learn to rely on a Gilbey's label. This meant that the firm could not specialize in the small products of small vineyards in special vintage years. They marketed standard brands. They had therefore to concentrate upon bulk purchases.

As pioneers of low-priced wines they had a certain amount of prejudice to overcome. Persons who had been in the habit of paying high prices for château-bottled clarets could not be easily persuaded that a cut in duty from one shilling to twopence a bottle admitted the importation of an immense quantity of pure, sound and palatable wine; cheapness to them was synonymous with inferiority. Moreover England, not being a wine-producing country, has the same snobbishness towards particular years and vineyards that Republican countries, possessing no title of nobility, have towards foreign noblemen. The English make a fetish about the classified growths of the Médoc in a way that the French themselves never do, proud though they are of their finest wines, and ready though they are to pay high prices for them. But the English will pay higher still, as can be seen in the prices of a château-bottled Margaux or Lafite of a good year. The connoisseurs of the eighteen-sixties were reluctant to admit that many excellent wines, whose inferiority to the classified growths only an expert could detect, could be obtained at a moderate price.

But in point of fact it was not the connoisseur clientèle that the Gilbeys were hoping to attract. Amateurs of wine whose cellars had been stocked for at least a generation by one or other of the old-established wine merchants were not likely to withdraw their custom in favour of what their conservatism might consider a brash price-cutter. The Gilbeys were aiming at a new class of wine-drinker, whom the low price of wine would induce to experiment with claret in preference to beer and spirits.

In their search to find the most suitable wines for this new public, they soon found that in wine as in other trades the steadiest profit is made by the middleman. They decided therefore to cut out that profit, and deal direct with the French wine growers.

At this stage they were most lucky in being able to draw not only upon the experience of Henry Parry Gilbey but upon his connections as a wholesale merchant. From the very start Henry Parry had taken a close personal interest in the new experiment. Day after day he would walk from his house in Brunswick Square on his way to the City and confer with and advise his younger brothers, in whose offices his trim beard and waxed moustache were soon as familiar as Walter's single eyeglass and slender elegance, and the more bohemian Alfred's bow-tie. Regarding his original loan as an investment, Henry had taken his share in the first profits, and he soon decided to throw in his lot completely with his family; in 1866 he resigned from his old firm, Southard, Gilbey & Co., and became a W. & A. Gilbey partner.

In the meantime—this was rather earlier—he was able to put his future colleagues in touch with the wine-producing markets.

In 1860 James Blyth had waited with his trunks packed to sail to the Cape. In 1863, already noted as a judge of wine and a keen businessman, he made his first tour with Alfred Gilbey through the French wine districts to make purchases and to establish contact with the growers. The direct relationships then formed have continued harmoniously ever since. Alfred Gilbey was the recorder of the trip. He entered the transactions and wrote up a diary. At the end of the day he was too tired for these exertions and used to leave his reports till the morning. He rose each day at four o'clock, and made by all accounts very heavy weather of it. He was not a fluent linguist and James Blyth used to complain at being woken up with frequent questions about foreign idioms.

These visits were repeated yearly, and every wine-producing country in Western and Central Europe was included in the itinerary. For the first time a large British retail business was brought into direct relations with the growers. As a result Gilbey's were able to dispense with the Continental agent. Becoming direct buyers, they reduced the expenses of transportation and gave their customers the advantage of reduced costs. They also obtained first-hand information about the prospects of individual vintages and vineyards, and were able to create a demand for types of wine scarcely known in England. They secured in fact an ascendancy in Continental markets that they have never lost, though the majority of their rivals later followed their example.

Every year one or other of the partners made a trip abroad and the confidential reports that are still treasured among the archives of the house show the thoroughness with which these investigations were undertaken. The following paragraphs from a report made in 1876 by Alfred Gilbey and James Blyth after a tour in Tarragona are typical of the minuteness of the information collected and the care taken to ensure that all the wines handled by the firm justified the descriptions on their labels.

(It should be remembered in reading the following paragraphs that the method of making red wines in Spain is somewhat different from that employed in France and Germany.)

We now desire to give you our general impressions of the district, its capabilities of producing wine, the varieties suitable for export, and the means we think should be adopted to purchase most economically the wines we require. Only a few years back the wines of Tarragona were consumed exclusively in their natural state like claret, and, after meeting the wants at home, the remainder of the enormous production was shipped chiefly to the Spanish possessions in America, just the same as a large quantity of natural wine goes from Lisbon and Oporto to the Portuguese possessions. In course of time, however, a demand for strong wine sprang up from these colonies, and spirits being easily obtainable, a wine was soon supplied to them inferior, no doubt, in quality to port, but much cheaper in price, and therefore it was not surprising that this wine should find its way to England after the reduction of duty in 1860. Previously, of course, it was excluded by a duty of *5s. 9d.* a gallon.

The close relationship and constant communication existing between Spain and her colonies, and the fact that over 100,000 pipes of Spanish red wines were annually shipped to the latter, have created constant applications for various descriptions of white and sweet wines, and a feeling naturally existing not to refuse business has caused Tarragona to become already, to a small extent, a depot for so-called *façon* wines. Therefore, in almost every establishment we have visited, besides tasting the natural produce of this district, we have had shown us, and sometimes with a certain amount of pride, wines labelled port, sherry, claret, madeira, etc., but grown in the Tarragona vineyards. . . .

With regard to the red wines of Tarragona, we believe the trade is only in its infancy, for the quantity produced is yearly increasing, and there is every prospect of the quality improving, as the farmers gain more understanding in the use of spirit in the earlier stages of fermentation. In this, our first visit, we have to confine our observations to the merchants, and although it has given us an excellent preliminary insight into the business, it has not provided us with all the information necessary to enable us to make purchases.

The Gilbeys were very thorough. Not only did they visit the wine-growing but the cork-growing districts, a knowledge of which is obviously important to the wine merchant. Modern science has found no effective substitute for the cork, and in the mid-nineteen-forties, when the frontier between France and

Spain was closed, the wine merchants found themselves in considerable difficulties. Corks fit for bottling must be taken from trees between thirty and forty years old—the earlier strippings being only fit for tanning, net floats and suchlike uses. The crop can only be taken at intervals of seven or ten years.

It is a complicated business and the following extract from a report by James Blyth and Charles Gold after a visit to Palafrugell is not without its interest:

> . . . We find that the whole of the Province of Gerona is devoted to the growth of the cork wood, the mountains being covered with the trees in all directions, which we observed on our journey here. It appears a very easy way for men to invest their capital, and peculiarly suited to the Spanish temperament, for very little supervision or outlay is necessary. As an instance, we heard of one proprietor of a cork forest who sold annually £3,000 worth of cork wood, and his only expense was £60 a year for 'stripping'. It is customary to strip a tree every seven or ten years, according to the pocket of the proprietor, but of course there are trees of every stage, so that it is an annual process which takes place in all the forests. An experienced eye can detect when a tree was last relieved of its bark. When you hear of the enormous quantities of corks annually exported, it would naturally seem that with its slow growth the stock would soon be exhausted; but we are told that only one-third of the cork forests of Spain are worked at all, the bulk of this kind of property being in the hands of noblemen of Spain.

There is an interesting family corollary to these frequent trips. The clan spirit has been strongly marked among the Golds and Gilbeys, the Blyths and Grinlings, and the intermarriage of first and second cousins has been so consistent a feature of the family tree that Major Vivian Nickalls—whose brother Guy, the famous Oxford oarsman, married a daughter of Henry Gold—wrote in his autobiography 'it would take the College of Heralds years to discover their various ramifications.' Three of Alfred Gilbey's sons during their journeys to Jerez allied themselves in marriage with Spanish ladies—themselves vaguely interrelated—thus introducing a Catholic element that has expanded in succeeding generations, the present Roman Catholic Chaplain of Cambridge University, Monsignor Alfred Newman Gilbey, being the great-grandson of the Essex coach proprietor, and a great-great-grandson, Peter Gilbey, is a monk in the Benedictine Order.

The business ties that were made during these first years have lasted unbroken for close upon a century. The House of Gilbey has had a constant and happy knack of converting bonds of business into bonds of friendship. The chief European houses with which the firm has been associated may be listed here:

Messrs. Gonzalez Byass of Jerez de la Frontera
Messrs. Thomas Hine of Jarnac Charente
Messrs. Louis Latour of Beaune, Côte d'Or
Messrs. Cossart Gordon of Madeira
Messrs. Croft of Oporto
Messrs. José Boule of Tarragona

In many cases subsequent ties of blood relationship have made these associations intimate. Perico Gonzalez, Marquis of Torre Soto, and William Crosbie Gilbey married sisters—the Gordons of Jerez of the Wardhouse family of Aberdeen; two Gonzalez sons married daughters of William Crosbie Gilbey; Newman Gilbey married a niece of the Marquis of Torre Soto; and Daniel Hine married Maud Gilbey, daughter of Walter Gilbey.

Within a short while so widespread had the Gilbey Empire become that the House was forced to set up extensive premises for their supplies. Great stocks were held in Jerez and Oporto and automatically replaced as they ran down. Visiting these various markets, the partners had a comfortable feeling of proprietorship without any of the responsibilities of actual ownership.

Gilbey's were always on the look-out for opportunities to enlarge their business, and it is interesting to note how often these opportunities came through a family link. In 1872 F. C. Frye, a relative of the first Mrs. Alfred Gilbey, started with his mother-in-law the partnership Leverett and Frye—a chain of licensed grocery shops, the first multiple company in this line. Gilbey's financed the company, feeling that it would provide a useful market for their wines, and, when Frye became M.P. for North Kensington, took over the entire business, which they eventually sold in 1916, though they retained the Irish branches.

It was through a family link that the house became interested in tobacco. A cousin of Mrs. Argo Gold's, David Abercrombie, was manager of R. J. Hill Ltd., who marketed tobacco for pipes and for self-rolled cigarettes. This proved a profitable side-line for a while, but Gilbey's failed to recognize that Wills and Players had in machine-made cigarettes a far more popular commodity. Gilbey's scoffed at them as a passing fashion, and a chance was missed. It is interesting to record the one occasion on which Gilbey's failed to recognize which way the tide was running.

Perhaps it was as well. The business in wines was the mainspring of the firm, and Gilbey's might not have prospered so quickly had their energies been dissipated over many interests before success was fully established. As it was, the 'sixties saw a remarkable consolidation. By the end of that decade the firm was well enough established to publish a cloth-bound book, *On Wines of the Principal Producing Countries.* Its nineteen chapters are still valuable for the shrewd comments they contain on wine in general and on wines in particular, and on the economic effects of national custom: this passage provides a good example:

> It may not be amiss to advert to . . . the results arising from the almost extreme minuteness of classification of the different wines of France. Unlike the produce of Spain and Portugal, where the contrary extreme prevails, and all wine . . . stands upon its own merit, independent of the district or grower by whom it is produced, French wines are divided into almost endless varieties, according to the name of the estate or district upon which they are grown.
>
> In one sense no doubt this system has its advantages, as it tends to produce a certain pride, and ensure an amount of care and attention in the keeping up of valuable names and qualities; but on the other hand it has likewise its drawbacks and disadvantages, as it has induced too great a reliance on the value of certain of the better known of these names, and has undoubtedly led to increased prices, founded simply on name and not intrinsic value, while it offers an inducement to bring into the market, under fictitious designation, wines of inferior value. By this system also the value of particular estates and vineyards is unduly enhanced, and attention is diverted from the undoubted merits of other but less known wines.

Château Loudenne in the Médoc

The Upper Douro Valley

Vintage at Roeda: Vintagers carrying grapes to the pressing

Roeda: Oxen in tr
tional harness

The firm was only a dozen years old, and yet the anonymous writer of Gilbey's book must have been able to reflect, as he penned the following passage, how much Gilbey's had pioneered the development he was recording, and how much it had profited in the process:

> There is no doubt that at the present time a knowledge of all that pertains to the subject of wine and the different wine-producing countries has a greater interest for the public than it has had at any previous period; while the different wine countries are now so thoroughly opened up by modern commerce, that we have an almost infinite variety to choose from, sufficiently varied indeed to meet every caprice of fashion or taste. Owing also to the fact that England has for many years been one of the best markets for wines, and that large stocks have always been held by merchants in London and at the out-posts, a check has been kept upon any great increase or variation in price, from insufficient vintages or increased demand; indeed at the present time it is a well ascertained fact that wines generally are cheaper in England relatively than in any other part of the world.

It might have been written of our own days, as also might this paragraph:

> The high rate of the wine duties, till within the last few years, has been such a bar to the use of wine in this country that its value and properties may be said to have been comparatively unknown up to the present period. The more recently inaugurated laws have, however, opened up wide fields from which the produce of the grape may be as conveniently brought within reach of the consumer in this country as on the Continent. The heavy restrictions imposed, in the shape of fiscal duties, have hitherto shut out from our ports an almost endless variety of cheap and wholesome wines, but of late it has become pretty generally understood that taxation may be lightened, not only in the interest of the foreigner, but to the advantage in many ways of the people at home; among which not the least important are a greatly increased temperance, and a variety of choice and taste to the consumer.

The great Radical's name is not mentioned in this passage, though it is elsewhere in the book, and what was said, gratefully, of Cobden in the eighteen-sixties might have been echoed, in the late nineteen-forties, of Sir Stafford Cripps.

CHAPTER IV

New Premises Are Found

THE treatise mentioned in the previous chapter *On Wines of the Principal Producing Countries*, bore on its title-page the announcement,

LONDON
Printed and Published by Walter and Alfred Gilbey
At the Pantheon, Oxford Street

—an early printed reference to a landmark in the history of the firm. As the Gilbey's enterprise steadily and continuously expanded, it was soon found that even the new premises in Titchfield Street were inadequate to the increased volume of business, and in 1867 the Pantheon was acquired.

The contemporary visitor to London will search Oxford Street in vain for that impressive building with its pillared portico which for seventy years was associated with the House of Gilbey, but in its day it was one of 'London's sights'.

First opened in 1772 as 'a place of evening entertainment for the nobility and gentry'—a winter counterpart to Ranelagh—its fortunes provide an interesting footnote to social history.

Three years earlier, while it was being built, Horace Walpole had written to Lady Ossory:

> What do you think of a Winter Ranelagh erecting in Oxford Road at the expense of £60,000? If we laugh at the French they stare at us. Our enormous luxury and expense astonish them. I carried their Ambassador and Comte de Levi to see the Pantheon, which is almost finished. Imagine Baalbec in all its glory. It amazed me. The pillars are of artificial giallo-antico. The ceilings, even of the passages, are of the most beautiful stuccos in the best taste of the grotesque. The ceilings of the ball-room and the panels are painted like Raphael's *loggias* in the Vatican. A dome like the Roman Pantheon, glazed. Monsieur de Guisnes said to me, '*Ce n'est qu'à Londres qu'on peut faire cela.*'

Small wonder that Horace Walpole was amazed. The fantastic James Wyatt was its architect, of whom John Summerson has written, in his *Georgian London*, that he was 'apparently destitute of any convictions whatever, moral or artistic, drink and women were his habitual employments, though he indulged at intervals in orgies of architectural designing.'

The Pantheon was the successful outcome of just such an orgy, for its glory was a domed cathedral-like hall, with double-storied aisles and rounded ends, curiously—for Georgian London—reminiscent of the original Pantheon in Rome, and of Santa Sophia in Constantinople. Summerson has said of it that:

> no interior so gorgeous had been built in London since Wren finished St. Paul's. . . . The Byzantine body, mantled in fine, restrained embroideries, must indeed have been a spectacle. The artificial lighting played up to the architecture and the flicker of candlelight quickened the chiaroscuro paintings into glimpses of Valhalla, while friezes and niches were accented with green and purple lamps and the dome swam in a heathen twilight, reflected from gilt vases.

At first, the proprietors, out of a resolve to be exclusive, refused to accept subscriptions to the Pantheon unless they came on the recommendation of a peeress, explaining that their desire was:

> to prevent such people only from obtaining Subscriptions whose Appearance might not only be improper, but subversive of that Elegance and Propriety which they wish on every occasion to preserve . . . by which Means those whose Situation and Character will entitle them to a Place amongst People of Fashion and

Politeness may, by applying at the Pantheon, be accommodated with Subscription.

The subscription was six guineas: the entertainments consisted of concerts, balls and masquerades. But the company had been chosen with too strict a regard for the proprieties and the proceedings in the Pantheon's very earliest days were decorous but dull. Not that the decorum lasted long: as soon as the Prince of Wales (the future George IV) began to patronize the masquerades, the temper of the evenings changed, the Pantheon became a huge success, and the *Morning Herald*, in its reports of the occasions that his presence graced, would conclude its list of the titled and untitled ladies who accompanied him with the statement that 'the Cyprian Sisterhood were most of them present'. Masked balls at the Pantheon were far less sedate by now than the pleasures of Ranelagh and by the time Charles James Fox was learning to be a man about town there were occasions when it was 'customary at the end of an indecorous masquerade to fling open the windows and pelt the eager, hungry, thirsty, and howling crowd below with hay, empty bottles and the remains of the supper'. It was an appropriate atmosphere for the one architectural masterpiece of a man of whom it has been written that when he was killed in a coaching accident in 1814, and buried in (of all places) Westminster Abbey, 'only his wickednesses were remembered.'

So the Pantheon became the centre of London's 'bright young people'; the public was admitted to the gallery; and Boswell's complaint that there was not a half-guinea's worth of pleasure in it merited Dr. Johnson's retort, 'But, Sir, there is half-a-guinea's worth of inferiority to other people in not having seen it.'

During the day it attracted custom more soberly by its exhibition of scientific apparatus, and the Prince of Wales was nearly killed by an imprudent meddling with a lightning conductor.

In 1790, the opera-house in the Haymarket having burnt down, Mr. O'Reilly took a lease of the Pantheon at an annual rent of £3,000, obtaining a licence from the Lord Chamberlain to call it the King's Theatre. It was opened for Italian Opera in February, in 1791, but was totally gutted by fire on January 14, 1792, nothing but Wyatt's walls being left standing. The shell was refitted as a theatre and place of general entertainment and reopened in February 1795. But it had lost its *chic.* The Royal Princes still frequented it, but by then the Royal Princes were themselves discredited in the eyes of the English aristocracy. It is recorded that in 1808 Louis XVIII, during his exile, paid a visit there but it was by daylight and to inspect a curiosity that was on show.

The fortunes of the Pantheon declined at a corresponding pace with the dignity and credit of its first patron. By the time the Prince Regent had become 'The First Gentleman in Europe', the Pantheon had become a third-class music hall. Its proprietors became involved in lengthy and costly litigation, and when at last the premises were put up for auction they were practically in ruins and fetched only £13,000. That was in 1832. Thirty-five years later the Gilbeys were to pay £67,000, but the building had in the meantime been refitted as a public bazaar and fine art gallery; a placid and relatively prosperous period, but the garish glamour of Regency's revels still lingered round the high arched ceiling and Palladian pillars.

Its acquisition had a definite value in prestige and publicity for a rising firm. It made its own special contribution to the firm's success; it made a 'talking point' for travellers and salesmen. Daily lunch parties were held there. It became a family rendez-vous, a central meeting place during a morning's shopping. It afforded a great post of vantage, all the Royal processions passing it on their way to the Guildhall: still in the memory of one member of the Board is the sight of the German Emperor, handsomely moustached, splendidly uniformed, and magnificently mounted, riding in Edward VII's funeral procession. The pictures that are included in this history will give a clear impression of the Pantheon's character—and show, too, how times had changed from the gay and lively indecorum of the Regent's day: look at the stiff collars and the side-whiskers, the obviously hushed attention to business, of the clerks at the Pantheon's desks in the 1907 photograph of the firm's head office!

The Pantheon was bought in 1867, but even this large building was soon not big enough to deal with the rapidly increasing volume of business, and as its cellars were found to be too dry for the storing of wine, it was decided to move the bottling stores to the premises at Camden Town which the firm still holds as tenants of British Railways, though the Pantheon remained the firm's administrative headquarters until the beginning of World War II.

'All great railway stations surround themselves with a sort of debatable land that is neither residential, commercial, industrial, trading, nor theatrical.' So wrote James Bone, in *The London Perambulator*, in a chapter he entitled 'North o' Euston'. And it was north of Euston that Gilbey's established not only their distillery but their complex of warehouses and bottling stores. It is a district strongly marked by the early years of the railway age, when the mile-long incline from Euston to Camden Town, a gradient of one in seventy, with the Regent's Canal to cross at the top, was too steep for locomotives, and trains were winched up by stationary steam engines working an endless rope.

Of Gilbey's buildings in this district, one—the present administrative and office building in Oval Road—was not built until 1937, but most of the remainder is property dating from these early days. In 1869 Gilbey's leased from the railway what was known then, and is still known, as 'A' shed (four floors each of two acres)—built in the eighteen-forties as a warehouse, where now bottling is carried out for the Home Trade.

Nearby is Gilbey's Cask Bond with a storage capacity of 6,000 casks and with blending vats holding over 60,000 gallons. Much of the space lies under Camden Town goods yard in long arcades formed by the typical series of 'railway arches' that were thought at one time to be necessary to support railways and rolling-stock, and that are to be found all over or, rather, all under London—dark and sinister, though admirably suited for the storage of wine on account of their constant temperature. Here are to be found butts of sherry holding their 108 gallons, and longer, narrower pipes of port holding 117 gallons; butts of whisky, and puncheons of rum with their respective half measures, hogsheads.

In adjacent warehouses are the bonded bottling stores where there are Customs officers on permanent duty, and where bottles are being filled and labelled that will join the cases already labelled for Bahrein and Mainz, Antwerp and Kuala Lumpur.

Most notably a memorial to the early railway age is the

Round House, built in 1847, scheduled for preservation by the Ministry of Housing and Local Government, and singled out in Nikolaus Pevsner's book on the buildings of London—160 feet in diameter, looking low for its size because of the great span of the circular slate roof, which is held on twenty-four slender cast-iron columns. It was originally a turntable house for locomotives—you can still see the tracks where the puffing billies in the eighteen-forties turned away from the steep slope down to Euston and prepared for the long haul north. Students of architecture come to draw this remarkable piece of design and construction, and have to be given permission by the Surveyor in charge of the permanent Customs guard, for here are fifteen monster vats of whisky, each worth about £140,000 (of which the forty is the whisky and the hundred is the duty), as well as row upon row of mere barrels of whisky, brandy and rum, all bonded and not yet having paid duty.

Spirits are drawn for distribution all over the world from this remarkable building, a link with the age when Gilbey's itself was born. To see the stocks here and in other warehouses—to tot up the value even on those that have not yet paid duty—is to realize the financial problems of a trade which has to lock up so much of its capital in assets that are liquid in everything but the financial sense.

CHAPTER V

Château Loudenne

THE Gilbeys went abroad to find new types of wine to satisfy the tastes of a new drinking public and one of the first rewards of that search was the introduction under its own name of the sparkling wine of Saumur.

In 1873 Alfred Gilbey and James Blyth had discovered that large quantities of cheap sparkling wines produced on the Lower Loire, as much as two hundred miles from the true champagne country, were being sold in England as champagne. They felt this practice to be unwise, yet at the same time they recognized that some of the sparkling wines produced in this area, though different from champagne, were in their own way excellent. They arranged therefore to put the best of them upon the English market under their own name and at a price which corresponded with the cost of their production. The experiment was successful and Saumur became popular.

Their most important step, however, was the purchase in 1875 of Château Loudenne, an estate of 470 acres that lies about thirty-five miles north of Bordeaux, in the heart of the Médoc. The property, which was then owned by La Vicomtesse de

Marcellus, was producing annually two hundred hogsheads of sound claret; it was clearly capable of very considerable development, but its vineyards could not hope to supply more than a fraction of the firm's great and rapidly increasing requirements. It was as a depot that it appealed principally to Alfred Gilbey and James Blyth. Buying upon the spot, they needed a collecting centre where they could store and prepare their wines. They also recognized the prestige they would acquire as owners of a château in the eyes of the Bordeaux shippers and proprietors. From now on, they would be regarded as 'one of us', and Alfred Gilbey wrote in his diary, 'Looking at Loudenne with the eye of a proprietor, grower and agriculturist and perhaps a little as we do at a parcel of wines when it has become our property, we felt more than pleased with our bargain.'

The estate was purchased for £28,000 and within a few years a further £64,500 had been invested in replanting, improvements and extensions. Gilbey's were at this time shipping annually to England six to seven thousand hogsheads, and they built a *chais*, which included a modern *cuvier* and cooperage, that was capable of holding sixteen thousand hogsheads. A small port was constructed on the river, with a tramway running to it from the *chais*. They also built workshops, workmen's cottages, and stables for horses and for oxen; so thorough was their resolve to exploit every aspect of their acquisition that in the hope of tapping water from the Pyrenees—a hope that was eventually to be disappointed—they sank an artesian well to a depth of 497 metres, more than 1,600 feet.

The Vicomtesse had kept only 60 acres of her property under cultivation, but by 1889 a further 125 acres had been planted with vines. The annual wage bill in 1875 was £500; by the turn of the century it was £7,000. By 1883 the annual production of wine had been raised from 200 to 500 hogsheads; a figure that was to be doubled within the next four years. As a tribute to this energy and enterprise, the French Ministry of Agriculture awarded the Château its Gold Medal in 1887 for the best managed vineyard in the Gironde; in 1900 a second Gold Medal was won at the Paris exhibition and in the following year it received the Gold Medal and Diploma from the Agricultural Society of the Médoc. As recently as 1954 the Château was still winning awards, among them a Gold Medal Diploma for efficient viticulture and for its white wine. Maurice Healy, in the book on claret which he contributed to Constable's Wine Library, spoke of Château Loudenne, after referring to its fermenting vats lined with glass, as an estate which its owners had 'sought with much success to make a model of what a vineyard should be'.

The purchase of Château Loudenne is one of the key events in the story of the House of Gilbey. Yet within a few months of the final signature, the partners must have wondered whether they had not made a mistake; or at least must have been tempted to regret their deal. For the French wine trade was then suffering the greatest calamity in its history, the attack on the vines from the *Phylloxera vastatrix*, a species of plant aphis, perhaps more easily recognized for what it is as a vine louse, first recorded in England at Kew, in 1863, soon to devastate the vineyards of Europe.

Economists estimated that the country suffered more financially from this scourge than it was soon to do from the losses of the Franco-Prussian War, and the new proprietors of Château Loudenne were put to enormous expense in combating the plague, first by soaking the soil with sulpho-carbonate and later by grafting European vines on to North American stock, which had become largely immune to the phylloxera, which is itself American in origin. Indeed, the Gilbeys were only able to survive the calamity through having ample capital available to meet a sudden drain. Many of the smaller estates were bankrupt. In 1886 Alfred Gilbey wrote in his diary that 'the small number of properties in the Bas Médoc which have escaped destruction could be almost counted on two hands', and two years earlier he had written that 'the sad state of affairs in the Bas Médoc on the properties of the small holders, in comparison with the healthy and productive appearance of the vineyards adjoining large estates, would afford the strongest argument which could be adduced against the establishment in England of small peasant proprietors as a measure against the present agricultural depression.'

During this period of crisis, the value of close personal

connections with the wine trade were amply proved. When phylloxera attacked the vines of Cognac, the brandy market was dislocated for many years. Yet Gilbey's were able to secure from the stocks of the principal growers brandies to the value of nearly a million pounds. The huge sum of money involved in this transaction shows both what an immense reserve of capital and credit the firm had built up in less than a quarter of a century, and how intimate a relationship had been established with the French wine merchants. On no other basis could Gilbey's have acquired at a time of scarcity so large a consignment of a rare commodity.

By the middle of the eighteen-eighties the phylloxera pest had been eliminated, and even if the new grafted vine had the disadvantage of a short life—some twenty-five to thirty years, as opposed to the century or so of the old native vine—the gentle slopes of the Médoc were green again.

The new post-phylloxera wines were to receive, however, at any rate in England, a somewhat different reception. For during the eighteen-eighties a definite change took place in the drinking habits of the English. Both the demand for claret and the price paid for it diminished. In 1876 over six and a half million gallons were imported into England; and in 1905 only three and a half, although the population had increased by a third, and no wave of temperance had swept the country.

It is probable that this decline in the drinking of Médoc wine can only partially be attributed to the ravages of phylloxera. Two other considerations, the prevalence of cigarette smoking, and a taste for whisky—particularly the medical belief in the curative efficacy of whisky—had their effect on English habits. In the eighteen-sixties the English had indulged in the habit, very puzzling to the French, of drinking their best claret after the meal. In Saintsbury's *Notes on a Cellar Book* the menus of the eighteen-sixties invariably have a red wine following champagne, though preceding port. And Frank Harris, who, though not the most reliable of witnesses, has his value as a guide to the social habits of the *fin de siècle*, refers in *My Life and Loves* to the abandonment during the 'nineties of the habit of drinking claret after dinner. He attributes this to the emancipation of women, and their refusal to allow their husbands to 'sit and soak' over their glasses till their servants carried them away. This is no doubt partly true, but the cigarette played an important part. A cigarette affects the palate and removes the wish to drink anything as delicate as claret. Virginia Cowles, in her account published in 1956 of the life and lively times of Edward VII, puts as early as the eighteen-seventies the decline of port drinking after dinner—and what is true of port was true, too, of claret. The Prince of Wales, she records, was the first host to permit smoking in the dining-room—after the ladies had withdrawn, of course—instead of restricting it to special smoking-rooms, to be enjoyed only in quilted jackets and with a tasselled cap to protect the hair from the smell of tobacco. Brandy stood up better than port to the rich, oily smell of Havana leaf, and brandy—Miss Cowles suggests—began as long ago as that to usurp some of the after-dinner status of port.

Monsieur André Simon gives another reason for the diminished consumption of claret, a reason that was a direct corollary to the phylloxera attack. As a result, good red wine was scarce in the eighteen-eighties; what little there was should consequently have been expensive, but a number of short-sighted shippers, in order to retain their customers, supplied inferior wines at the earlier price. The poor quality of this wine destroyed the confidence both of the wine buyers and the public.

Moreover, at the very time when the scourge of the phylloxera was rendering difficult the enjoyment of good claret, dry champagne was making its first appearance on the market. Dom Pierre Perignon may have invented sparkling wine in the late seventeenth century, but it was not till a modest chemist of Chalons-sur-Marne published in 1836 a booklet on the technique of controlling the carbonic acid gas produced in a bottleful of fermenting wine that the champagne industry became organized. Up till that point the average loss through exploding bottles varied between 25 and 40 per cent, so that still red and white wines were a more profitable investment for the Epernay wine growers. No large stocks were produced until the technique of production was finally established; it was not till the eighteen-sixties that a general taste for dry wine developed and champagne in England ceased to be a dessert or ladies' wine. W. E. Gladstone, a temperate man, drank a quart habitually with his dinner, and the consumption rose from seven million bottles in 1861 to twenty-one million in 1890.

In this connection it is interesting to note the drinking habits of the Forsytes in the first volume of the Saga. John Galsworthy was himself vividly appreciative of the pleasures of the table. His man-of-the-world characters pride themselves upon their palates. All the Forsytes except James, and he kept a fashionable table, were good trenchermen. They appear to have drunk nothing but champagne; they had port and brandy, sherry and madeira: but champagne was their table wine. Swithin Forsyte, in his last days deaf and stertorous, had always beside him on the dinner table in his club a steaming ice bucket. The two most memorable meals in Galsworthy are the Stoic's last dinner, and the dinner given by Soames and Irene Forsyte to June and Bosinney. At the first Old Heythrop drank several subsidiary drinks; he had sherry with his soup—complaining that 'no one drank sherry nowadays, hadn't the constitution for it'—although he had previously drunk a glass of champagne with his oysters; with his cheese savoury he had a glass of port, a '68. Finally he had brandy. But champagne was his table wine.

Champagne, of an unspecified year and shipper, was the wine chosen by Soames Forsyte for his cousin and her fiancé. The dinner is remarkable, if not indeed unique in literature, as being both one of the most succulent meals served on the printed page, and an occasion of the most acute embarrassment. Rarely can a meal have been chosen with greater care; rarely can a meal have provided less enjoyment. The dinner is also interesting as an example of the quantity and the elaborateness of the food provided at this time for the English upper middle classes. It was a meal, it will be recalled, prefatory to a theatre. Soup came first. 'Bosinney, a glass of sherry with your soup.' Then a fine fresh Dover sole: cutlets 'each pink frilled', spring chicken, asparagus; an apple charlotte. Olives from France and Russian caviare were set upon small plates. Brandy accompanied Turkish coffee and Egyptian cigarettes. June and Bosinney went to the theatre by bus. Three minutes' walk from Montpelier Square to the

Brompton Road: at least fifteen minutes by horse bus to Piccadilly. One wonders at what time the meal began. There were of course no cocktails then. There was *le mauvais quart d'heure* instead.

Galsworthy was clearly at great pains about that menu. It is a little surprising that Soames in his own house should not have 'led up' to a big wine. He preferred, however, to serve champagne right through the meal. Clearly at that time the Forsyte classes considered that they could only trust one wine. It is a point worth stressing in a record such as this, for the fortunes of the House of Gilbey had been based on the success of 'Gladstone's claret'.

This recession in the demand for claret did not, however, affect their fortunes. They had by then several other irons in the fire and Château Loudenne was in no sense a white elephant. They had a ready market for all the wine it produced and they could store in their new *chais* as much or as little wine as the market needed. In 1890, for example, they bought two-thirds of the Pontet-Canet growth, 600 hogsheads at 850 francs a tun.

The diaries begun by Alfred Gilbey and continued by his successors, extracts from which are preserved at Château Loudenne in three large leather-bound albums, throw a series of interesting sidelights on the fluctuations of the claret trade up till the first world war. In 1891 a group of leading shippers are discussing methods of resuscitating the claret trade in England; in 1909 the introduction of Algerian wine is threatening to revolutionize the wine trade, and legislation is demanded. The diaries also show how important a place the Château played in the firm's social life.

Every September there were large gatherings from London for the *vendange*, and it would have been hard to find a more charming setting for a house party. The Château has charm, dignity and intimacy; it is long and low, of faded rose-coloured stone, slate roofed, with a rounded tower at each end. From its long stone-flagged terrace, that is in shade after the early morning, you look across a quarter of a mile of lawns and vineyards to the broad, brown river and the boats, large and small, that ply between Bordeaux and the Atlantic. Long avenues have been driven through the woods, and in 1885, to celebrate the tenth year of ownership, five thousand roses were planted before the high, arched gateway. Bowered in roses, and set in elms, the Château crowns a little hill from which can be seen the spires of thirteen churches, in which pious Bordelais give thanks for the gift of wine.

CHAPTER VI

Whisky Becomes Popular

IT has been suggested in an earlier chapter that a taste for whisky was partly responsible in the eighteen-eighties for the reduced consumption of claret. In Dickens, whisky is scarcely mentioned. 'B and S' (brandy and soda) was the drink for the smart man about town, if he felt like spirits rather than anything as light as hock-and-seltzer. Whisky was something barbarous from across the border, and until the eighteen-eighties it was more likely to mean Irish than Scotch—in 1875 Gilbey's sold 83,000 dozen Irish to only 38,000 dozen Scotch.

But as soon as the English became familiar with the excellence of Scotch whisky, and as improvements in distilling methods were introduced throughout the eighteen-seventies and eighties, its popularity increased so rapidly that a foreigner today invariably caricatures an Englishman with a whisky and soda or a tankard of bitter in his hand.

The juxtaposition is not inappropriate. For what brandy is to wine, whisky is to beer; the one obtained by distilling wine, the other by distilling fermented grain. To each, moreover, has the same generic name been applied, brandy being called *eau de vie* and the word 'whisky' (or, in Ireland, 'whiskey') being derived from the Celtic *uisge-beatha*, later *usquebaugh*, meaning 'water of life'.

The oldest reference to whisky appears in the Scottish exchequer rolls for 1494, where a Friar John Cor is issued eight bolls of malt wherewith to make *aquavitae*: and Burns, in his 'Tam o' Shanter', pays tribute in the same couplet to twopenny ale and to whisky:

> Inspiring bold John Barleycorn!
> What dangers thou canst make us scorn!
> Wi' tippenny, we fear nae evil:
> Wi' usquabae, we'll face the Devil!

Just as wine varies according to the soil and climate in which it is produced, so does whisky. Each country's product is completely different. Many countries have tried by using identical methods to produce a so-called 'Scotch' but without success. The soft burn water off the peaty moors of the Highlands and the peat reek give true whisky its inimitable flavour.

To the average contemporary Englishman 'whisky' means Scotch whisky. There has never been a great demand in England for either Canadian or Australian whisky. American whiskies have rarely found their way to the English table, and though Irish whiskey was popular in the eighteen-sixties, and there are still many who appreciate its special qualities, most connoisseurs would agree that only the best Bourbon whisky from Kentucky can enter into competition for flavour, richness and purity with the malt whiskies of Campbeltown and Speyside.

In the opinion of Mr. S. H. Hastie it was the Irish spreading northwards through Kintyre who introduced the Scots to the excellence of pot-distilled whisky. He dates the innovation to the middle of the eighteenth century, and certainly by the last quarter of that century an English import duty of 9*s*. 6*d*. a gallon had made the illicit distilling and smuggling of whisky one of the chief industries of the Highlands.

Few illicit industries have been more fortunately placed. For not only did the Highlands provide with their water, peat and barley the perfect ingredients for distilling whisky, but the remoteness of their glens provided the perfect cover for illicit stills. Nor is the process of manufacture complicated. It consists, in the simplest terms, of malting the barley, mashing the malt, fermenting the resultant liquor (the wort) into wash and finally submitting it to two pots for distillations. It is then filled into casks for maturing.

The popularity of Scotch whisky was a sudden growth. In 1879, so great were the fears that the phylloxera would mean that there was not enough wine to distil into brandy, that the brothers Gilbey invested almost a million pounds in all the cognac they could lay their hands on, pledging all their assets and taking out huge life insurances to do so. Brandy was so popular that steps as drastic as this had to be taken to safeguard supplies and stocks. But by 1886 the gold labels on Gilbey's Irish and Scotch whiskies, both labelled 'Castle Grand', and both selling at three-and-sixpence a bottle, were as familiar as their brandy labels. There was no denying the insistent demand for Scotch whisky, which had grown up in less than a decade, and in 1887, the year of the Golden Jubilee, Gilbey's applied to the sale of whisky the principle they had long applied to the sale of wine, of cutting out the middleman as far as possible, and dealing direct from the château, so to speak—in this case, the distillery—to the customer. They purchased the Glen Spey Distillery, in the famous Glenlivet district of Strathspey.

Eight years later, in October 1895, they bought the Strathmill Distillery, and in January 1904, the Knockando Distillery, both in the same district of Glenlivet. From these three distilleries the annual output is now nearly 300,000 gallons of proof spirit. At first Gilbey's refused to admit that anything but pure malt could be called 'Scotch whisky', but it was gradually appreciated that malt whisky was too heavy for a southern climate, and from 1905 they have added grain whisky to their blends.

At the same time the demand for Irish whiskey was not neglected. The difference in taste between the two types is marked. There are some who maintain that Irish whiskey bears a resemblance to the best American rye. There are also differences in the method of manufacture: Irish distilleries showing a preference for three distillations as against the two used in Scotland. Irish whiskey is made from a wider range of cereals and takes longer to mature in wood.

To meet the demand for Irish whiskey Gilbey's made an arrangement with the well-known firm of John Jameson & Son under which they now hold, in their bonded warehouses in Dublin, a larger stock of John Jameson's whiskey than any other firm in the world. Gilbey's brand of Red Breast twelve-year-old is the Irish equivalent of the famous Spey Royal Scotch whisky.

Later, as a corollary to their development of overseas distilleries, they established their own plants in Canada and Australia for the production of local whiskies. Slightly different methods were employed and no attempt was made to imitate the bouquet or the taste of Scotch. Each brand stood on its own feet and was destined for a particular market, in the country of its origin.

This period—the decade that saw the purchase of Château Loudenne and of a million pounds' worth of brandy, and that was on the eve of the great development of the firm's trade in whisky—saw, too, the death of one of the original partners. Alfred Gilbey, the youngest, had always been the most delicate of the brothers and he died suddenly, of pneumonia, at forty-six. The other original partners will be considered in a later chapter, but Alfred was the first to die, and he must be remembered in his appropriate place in this history. At the time of his death the partners were his two brothers; two nephews—James Blyth and Henry Arthur Blyth (sons of his sister, Caroline); two brothers-in-law, Henry and Charles Gold; and a cousin, Henry Grinling.

By the time of the purchase of Glen Spey these seven original partners had been joined by five of the second generation: Alfred's sons, Alfred, William Crosbie, and Newman; Walter's son, Henry Walter; and Henry Gold's son, Alfred Gilbey, or 'Argo'. Walter's second son, Arthur Nockolds, was to join the firm soon afterwards, in 1890. By that date, too, Gilbey's list quoted 192 brands of wine and 78 of spirits and liqueurs: one in every seventeen bottles of wine and one in every forty-two bottles of spirits consumed in the United Kingdom bore a Gilbey's label. The firm had travelled a long way in Alfred's short lifetime, and the next generation was maintaining the rate of progress.

CHAPTER VII

Sherry, Madeira, Port

IT was during the eighteen-sixties that the Gilbeys, whose first fortunes, it must always be remembered, were based on 'Gladstone claret', began to specialize in port and sherry—wines that are essentially different from what are usually called beverage or table wines in that they are fortified with brandy, a process which, in the case of port, checks fermentation from turning the whole of the grape-sugar content into alcohol. A further effect of the addition of brandy is that wines thus fortified will not deteriorate within a few hours of being opened, so that they can be left standing in an opened bottle, or in a decanter, for a week or longer.

Port and sherry—and with them are to be included madeira and marsala—have long been popular in England, their concentrated warmth and strength being particularly suited to a damp, chill climate.

There is no dated bottling with sherry, which is produced on the 'solera' system, a method of storing and maturing peculiar to the sherry-producing districts. The same casks are used from one vintage to the next; a collection of these casks is known as a solera, which is kept in bodegas, long open-air buildings, and never moved. The number of casks depends on the required output, as only a fifth of the total is available each year. The wine is gradually drawn off from the bottom tiers of casks, to be replenished from the top.

With sherry you have to trust your wine merchant. You tell him whether your preference is for a dry, a sweet, a light or a dark wine and he will accommodate you. The wine list in a country restaurant can tell you little. Amontillado should be pale and dry, Oloroso and Amoroso should be dark and full. But you can have no other guarantee of quality than the good name of the shipper.

Madeira also is a wine that has long been popular in England. The late Sir Stephen Gaselee was the most ardent of its recent advocates. Madeira retains its quality both in wood and bottle longer than any other wine. It takes a long while to mature and during the probationary period the casks are baked and rocked to prevent the wine from settling. In the days of sail it was used as ballast, the vintners maintaining that its quality was improved both by the rocking of the sea and by exposure to tropic suns. Casks that had been subjected to this experience were known as *vinho de roja* (travelled wine).

There are two schools of thought as to the place that madeira should occupy in the menu. There are many who hold, as Gaselee did, that it should start a meal, preferably with turtle soup; while others argue that it is too strong and sweet and should be served as a dessert wine either before or instead of port. There is a dryish madeira, *sercial*, but it has not proved as popular as the full-bodied *bual*. There is also a sugary Malmsey, but it was probably, in view of the date, in Cypriot Malmsey that 'false, fleeting, perjured' Clarence was drowned. Madeira is often dated, but the date upon a bottle is an indication of age rather than of a distinctive quality. With madeira as with sherry, the year of vintage has no significance.

It is for port that this particular distinction is reserved; and no wine fills a prouder and more honoured position at the English table. No wine is so truly English.

The Englishman and his port; what a world of Galsworthian tradition those five words evoke: of London clubs, and college

Vintage at Roeda:
Girls picking grapes

Strathmill Distillery, Speyside

Pot Stills, Glen Spey Distillery, Glenlivet

Malting Floor, Knockando Distillery, Speyside

Glen Spey Distillery and River Spey

Whisky Bottling Tanks, Bonded Warehouse, Edinburgh

common rooms and 'stately homes'; the pipe laid down at a son's christening, the cool dark cellars where the wine matures, the ritual of decanting, the bottle carried from the bin with cradling care, the muslin across the funnel's mouth, the light under the shoulder of the bottle; finally the strict conventions of the actual drinking, the decanter that must pass always to the left—clockwise, or the way of the sun—the cigarette that must remain unlighted.

Many tributes have been paid in literature to this noble wine. George Meredith's in *The Egoist* is the happiest, and a wine merchant might do worse than send to his customers as a Christmas card the twentieth chapter of that now neglected comedy. It has the much quoted phrase in reference to the crust that great wines throw, 'old wine, my friend, denies us the full bottle'. A phrase that is followed by the perfect duologue between guest and host:

> 'Another bottle is to follow.'
> 'No!'
> 'It is ordered.'
> 'I protest.'
> 'It is uncorked.'
> 'I entreat.'
> 'It is decanted.'
> 'I submit.'

The perfect juxtaposition of pressure, reluctance and gracious, grateful and well-timed surrender.

The same chapter contains the happiest definition of a cellar: 'Cellars are not catacombs. They are if rightly constructed, rightly considered cloisters where the bottle meditates on joys to bestow, not on dust misused.'

But it is in his weighing of the separate excellences of port and burgundy that Meredith crosses the border-line between prose and poetry.

> 'Hocks, too, have compassed age. I have tasted senior hocks. Their flavours are as a brook of many voices: they have depth also. Senatorial port! we say. We cannot say that of any other wine. Port is deep-sea deep. It is in its flavour deep; mark the difference. It is like a classic tragedy, organic in conception. An ancient Hermitage has the light of the antique; the merit that it can grow to an extreme old age; a merit. Neither of Hermitage

nor of Hock can you say that it is the blood of those long years, retaining the strength of youth with the wisdom of age. To port for that! Port is our noblest legacy! Observe, I do not compare the wines: I distinguish the qualities. Let them live together for our enrichment; they are not rivals like the Idaean three. Were they rivals, a fourth would challenge them. Burgundy has great genius. It does wonders within its period; it does all except to keep up in the race; it is short lived. An aged burgundy runs with a beardless port. I cherish the fancy that port speaks the sentences of wisdom. Burgundy sings the inspired ode. Or put it, that port is the Homeric hexameter, burgundy the Pindaric dithyramb. What do you say?'

'The comparison is excellent, sir.'

'The distinction, you should remark. Pindar astounds. But his elder brings us the more sustaining cup. One is a fountain of prodigious assent. One is the unsounded purple sea of marching billows.'

In 1952 I had the good fortune to be accorded a supreme example of the ceremony that attends the drinking of vintage port. I was one of a group of writers taken out by Gilbey's to Portugal to see the vintage.

In Oporto we were entertained to dinner at the Factory House, the hundred-and-fifty-years-old club for the member firms of the British Association of Port Shippers. Forty of us sat down to an excellent straightforward dinner; a dry white port as an aperitif, a white Graves preparing the way for a Pontet-Canet 1929, cheese straws cleaning the palate for a tawny port. At that point, so the menu informed us, we were to be offered two vintage ports, a 1917 and a 1927. The chairman rose to his feet. The bouquet of vintage port could not, he told us, be properly appreciated in an atmosphere that was tainted with the fumes of food; would we move into the adjoining room, bringing our napkins with us. There a second table awaited us, set with forty places.

It was a lovely sight, a gleaming stretch of mahogany under a cluster of chandeliers, bowls of red roses, high piled fruit; a Doulton dessert service, cut-glass decanters, a cherry-coloured carpet to match the china; a delight to the eye, but an even greater delight to the senses of touch and smell. It is always difficult, if not impossible, to describe a physical sensation; it is enough to say that coming into that cool-fresh room, its air scented with fruit and flowers, I had the sense of being transported to another planet; a moment later I was thinking, 'I'm living in another century.'

It was a feeling that I had often during the next few days. In the previous autumn I had seen the *vendange* at Bordeaux; there I had been struck by the changes that have taken place in recent years. The cultivation of the vineyard—ploughing, hoeing, ridging, spraying and, of course, haulage, is now done entirely by machine, which has ousted the horses and oxen of the past. The founding partners of the firm who bought Loudenne would have rubbed their eyes to see a thirty-horsepower tractor winding its way through the vines. But they would have recognized and understood the actual making of the wine—for there the traditional methods are best and have survived.

It all looked very calm and leisurely in the bland autumn light. Very few people seemed to be employed: nobody was hurrying. It was very different in the Douro.

Our party was taken to Quinta da Roeda at Pinhao. By rail it is under a hundred miles from Oporto, but the road winds along the steep hills that flank the Douro, rising at the Marao Pass to a height of 3,000 feet, and the journey took five hours. Much of the countryside appears barren, with only olive and cork trees flourishing in that slaty soil—schistose is the geologists' word for it—and with an occasional pine tossing its feathered head-dress. But as one climbs, one reaches areas of recent afforestation. There is considerable terracing, and the tiny hamlets on the way are as charming as they are lovely. Smoke curls through the tiled roofs of the cottages, scenting the air with the smell of the brushwood that burns under many an old iron pot.

Portugal produces a great deal of table wine for its own consumption, 'bigger' and coarser than comparable French wines, but highly palatable; and vineyards line the roads. *Vinho verde*—green wine—is a young wine that is very popular on local tables; it is slightly fizzy, it has a mere nine per cent content of alcohol, and is refreshing in hot weather; it also balances the heavy Portuguese diet whose basis is oil and rice and beans. Wine is plentiful along the Douro, but by official demarcation the wine of only one small area can carry the name of Port: there, the manufacture of the dessert wine is restricted by the Casa do

Douro, the official body that controls the district, so as to avoid over-production. Licences are granted yearly to the farmers, specifying the amount of wine that can be made into port, and the necessary brandy is allocated accordingly.

The wine not made into port remains as table wine, referred to as Douro Consumo, a good deal of which is taken over by the Casa do Douro for distilling into brandy—which will be used, in its turn, for the making of port. Generally speaking, the actual Douro district is divided by the river Corgo, immediately above the chief town of the district, Regoa. Wines from below the Corgo, where quantity is achieved, are referred to as Baixo Corgo. Ports of quality come from Cima Corgo, 'above the Corgo'.

The Douro district is a narrow stretch of territory, roughly a hundred miles in length. It has been called Portugal's gold ring: if that is so the Quinta da Roeda might almost be called its diamond, for it lies in the very centre of the Cima Corgo.

The word *quinta* means farm, and there is nothing elaborate about any of the *quintas* that you will see dotted along the hill-side of the Douro with their names standing out in large black lettering against the long low white-painted walls. Even now, after the extensive rebuilding and replanning of the past thirty years, Quinta da Roeda is still a modest-seeming property—a one-storied bungalow, set about with its outhouses. But the house, offices and staff living quarters are new; the lodge where the wine is made and collected has been rebuilt and extended, and there are new farm buildings and stabling for the oxen. Tunnels have been driven into the side of the hill for water, and pumping machinery lifts water from the river to irrigate the staff's vegetable garden. The *quinta* produces above two hundred pipes of port a year, and above twenty pipes of olive oil.

The permanent staff is small: only about twenty or so, but the dormitories are nearly always full; except for six weeks in late July and August, there is work to be done among the vineyards: the spraying, the weeding, the grafting, the general maintenance of the roads and terraces, and it is one of the peculiarities of the Douro that there should be separate workmen for each particular operation, specially recruited, and that after their month or six weeks at the *quinta* they should return to their own village to attend to their own fields and spend the money they have earned. For the vintage itself, a mixed gang of men and women is recruited.

The vintage takes place at the beginning of October and it is the region's festal period. For a *quinta* like Roeda, a foreman will collect forty men and women, sometimes from his own, sometimes from neighbouring villages. It will be the same foreman every year, bringing the same team with him. They arrive like schoolchildren back for the holidays. They have travelled on foot as much as thirty miles over a rough road; but their entrance will have a ballet-like quality: they will be in two separate lines, of men and women, in single file: they will move at a quick jog, a musician at their heads, playing an accordion, a whistle or a flute. The women will be carrying their personal possessions on their heads in identical wicker baskets under a black shawl; the men carrying hoes over their shoulders to steady the baskets; they shout and sing and wave as they move into what will be their living quarters for the period of the vintage; the men and women, even if they are married, occupy separate quarters.

This atmosphere of ballet is continued right through the *vindima*. It is a period of exceedingly hard work: all day long the women are in the vineyards, picking the grapes under the brilliant sun. The baskets in which the men carry the grapes to the *lagars* weigh 130 lb. Whereas in the past wine was made by continual treading, nowadays treading is limited to the 'first-cut' (*corte*) that pulps the grapes. After that all pressing is done with wooden appliances.

Everything goes to music. The men carrying baskets move in line, at a jog-trot, as Africans do, to keep the weight off their feet, with a musician blowing the time for them on a whistle. There is a special music for the men working in the *lagars*, and in the evenings, when the girls come down and dance till midnight, the music gets keener as the men in the *lagars* are refreshed with tots of *bagaciera*—a potent brandy. The vintagers do not only look as though they were having the time of their lives: they are in fact having it. It is the big three weeks of their year. When working for the port shipper, they are better fed than at any other time. They have comfortable quarters: they have their litre of wine with every meal. It is a break with the routine of their existences; they meet old friends and make new ones. It is a great courting time. The joke about 'June babies' may not be founded on too strong a basis of fact, but many marriages can trace their origin to the evenings of the *lagars*.

They leave, as they arrive, with an air of ballet. The girls parade before the *quinta*, in single file, their spokesman at their head carries a *Rama*, a symbolic wand decorated with grapes and paper flowers, which she presents to the lady of the house with a flourish of *viva's*—'*Viva Portugal*', '*Viva Inghilterra*', '*Viva Quinta da Roeda*'. There is a fine litany of names and finally with a charming candour she shouts '*Viva myself*'. I fancy that I shall always enjoy vintage port and the ritual that goes with it the more for having seen the ritual and happiness that are the prelude to its long passage from the stalk upon the vine to the rich dark wine that twenty years later is reverently brought up from the cellar.

The same ritual exists in all the other *quintas*. With one or two exceptions, all the big shippers who are members of the British Association of Port Shippers have their own *quinta*, but they use it as a centre of operations, for the amount of wine produced on a shipper's own *quinta* bears little relation to his total requirements, and he buys a great proportion of his yearly total from Douro farmers, often from families he, or his own family, has known for generations. The shipper will usually buy the whole of a farmer's production whilst it is still on the vine, sending a foreman to superintend the picking of the grapes and the making of the wine.

One of the chief responsibilities of a shipper is the supervision of the various estates. He checks the cleanliness of every piece of equipment in a farmer's *adega*. The *lagars* in which the wine is made, the vats in which it is stored, pumps and all minor pieces of equipment are inspected. In checking the vats the foreman always observes the ritual of putting his head through the small slit in the head of the vat, and beating with his hand, or with a 'flogger', upon its side to stir up the air inside, so that he can test its aroma. Any acidity or uncleanness shows itself immediately. If you followed his example you would be surprised at the extent to which your nostrils would be stung by the powerful bouquet of wine with which the wood is soaked.

There is no equivalent here for the local co-operatives of the Bordeaux districts; and it is fascinating in vintage time as one strolls through a quiet village to turn a corner and see through a dark archway a couple of peasants making their vintage.

Yes, it was all like living in another century. And there are those who will argue that in the middle of the twentieth century, in a mechanized age, grapes should be pressed by machine, and not carried on men's shoulders up and down steep slopes, that lorries should replace the oxen with the curious bowler-hat padding between their horns—their harness is so arranged that they push their load instead of pulling—in the same way that lorries and the Douro railway have largely displaced for the purposes of transporting to Oporto the curious flat-bottomed square-sailed boats (*barcos rabelos*) that alone, in the old days, could satisfactorily navigate the shallow Douro and which are now perhaps maintained chiefly for reasons of sentiment. One day the peasants of the Douro may grow weary of their work in the vineyards; the young people may want to live in cities, and a shortage of labour may enforce the installation of machinery. One hopes that that day is distant. The port might lose its flavour, and certainly the life of the Douro will be the poorer without the festal weeks when the grapes are plucked and pressed.

The vintage takes place late in September and early in October. In February the wine is brought down the river either by boat or rail to the shippers' lodges at Oporto which are now concentrated on the south bank of the river at Vila Nova de Gaia, where it is measured, tasted, analysed, blended according to type and to the shipper's requirements, and then stored in casks to mature. Here the real work begins. If the wine of a certain year is found to be of exceptional quality and the shipper decides to call it a vintage year, then he will allocate a portion of the vintage, the 'pick', to be shipped eighteen months later, to England, to be bottled—the corks being branded with the date and his name.

The shipper has done his task, and much now depends on the bottler, and on his experience and loving care. The bottler rests the wine and chooses the right moment to bottle it. He corks, capsules and waxes the bottles. It takes specialized cellarmen, too, to bin the wine into its resting place, where it will mature quietly in the dark, safe from oxidization, throwing its crust, perhaps for twenty or thirty years.

The bottler of a vintage port should have his bottling completed before the second Christmas following the vintage—in a little over a year, that is.

With duty today at 100*s.* a dozen, where once it was 16*s.*, the Government permits traders to bottle their wines in a special bonded department in a Duty Paid Store, paying duty only when the wine is withdrawn for sale—an important concession when it is realized what the compound interest would mean over some ten or twenty years.

The wine that matures in wood—destined not to be 'vintage' port but ruby or, as it loses its colour, tawny—presents a very different problem. Oxygen seeps through the wood: the wine loses its alcoholic strength, it needs to be refreshed, it needs something to feed upon, and it has to be replenished with more wine. The problem of the shipper is a constant one: he has to maintain on the market a constant homogeneity of taste, and colour, for his different brands. Gilbey's 'Old J' and 'Triple Crown' brands must always look and taste the same. Otherwise the customer would reasonably complain that the wine differed in quality or type, bottle from bottle.

This homogeneity can only be maintained by constant care and accurate blending in the hands of experts; absolute uniformity can be maintained from a shipper's stocks over an incredibly long period. This is not surprising when it is realized that Gilbey's hold stocks in Portugal and in bond in London worth almost a million pounds. It is not till a wine has been eight years in cask that it loses its ruby and gradually acquires its tawny colour; until then it is shipped as a ruby port, excellent in its way, but with the inadequacies of all young wines. A tawny port is probably at its greatest after twelve years in wood; by that time even an expert could not tell of what wines it had been blended, and in what proportions. These tawny ports, aged in wood, are lighter than vintage ports, and more popular. Being freshly bottled, they should be ready to serve at any time, in brilliant condition, a pleasure to the eye, as to the palate.

The care of wine in cask for a dozen years involves endless labour and it is fascinating to go round the lodges and see the men at work on their various tasks. The lodgeman goes round the casks tapping them with a small wooden mallet on a long shaft. He can tell by the sound whether the level of the wine has sunk below the standard height. Samples are taken by means of a large pipette (valanche) for examination. A lodge like Croft's would keep a hundred and twenty men in permanent employment; sons succeed fathers for generations.

In the cooperage the casks are dismantled, cleaned and repaired. The casks are rocked backwards and forwards by two men. There is a chain inside the cask which acts as an abrasive in removing any solid deposit adhering to the staves. The deposits loosened by the chain are flushed out by jets of boiling water. The cooper, a true craftsman, who serves a long apprenticeship, goes round the casks before use with a light and a hammer looking for any defect.

Tawny port is as different from vintage port as claret is from burgundy. They are both great wines, they are both expensive, because they involve locking up capital for a long time. I fancy that those who prefer burgundy to claret will prefer vintage to tawny port. I have always been a burgundian myself and during my four wineless years in the Middle East during the war, I would reflect on those famous vintages, '22, '24, '27, '35, that were quietly maturing for me in an English cellar.

But my greater love of burgundy has not detracted from my enjoyment of Bordeaux wines, and a glass of old tawny, particularly at the end of lunch, has always seemed to me one of fate's kindlier gifts to man.

CHAPTER VIII

Personalities

IT is not the function of this book to paint character portraits of the partners. But Gilbey's has always been so exclusively a family business, the members of the house have always taken so great a pleasure and pride in the achievements of their colleagues, that it is pertinent to note at this point to what a marked extent the original partners made their marks in public life.

Particularly is this true of Walter Gilbey. A sportsman, a clubman, the friend of royalty, a lavish and a courteous host, he was one of the last great eccentrics. Inheriting from his coachman father a love of horseflesh, buying his first horse in Gallipoli from his winnings at cribbage, when he was little more than a lad himself, he looked on the hours he spent at a city desk as the purchase price demanded by his hobbies.

They were expensive hobbies, and proof of the speed at which the firm's fortunes prospered lies in the extent to which he could indulge them. As early as 1864 he was able to move out of London and fish the Stort. He would drive from the Pantheon to Epsom on Derby Day, in a carriage with four grey horses and an outrider, drawing all eyes in Oxford Street. By 1879 he was living back in the familiar Essex countryside at Elsenham, rearing some of the best livestock in the country, amassing a remarkable collection of sporting trophies, pictures and cups, and publishing a number of books upon his special subjects. His *Animal Painters of England*, published in 1900, drew largely for its illustrations on his collection, and his *Early Carriages and Roads*, published in 1903, is scarce now and a collector's item. He specialized in agricultural draught horses, and the high standard of quality among shire-horses can be traced in large part to the small company he formed in 1877 for the purchase of two Old English cart-horse stallions.

Three years later, having paid 900 guineas—at that time a very high price indeed—for the stallion Spark, he founded his own shire-horse stud. And the result of his example and labour is apparent today in the massive but gentle-eyed animals which have replaced the undersized, underfed work horses, with their ragged quarters and drooping ears, which served English farmers in the eighteen-sixties.

Not only did he improve the breed, but he did a great deal to improve the treatment of the cart-horse. He founded the London Cart Horse Society, instituting an annual Whit Monday Parade, which *Punch*, on May 23, 1891, celebrated in a poem containing the four lines:

> First-rate English horses in holiday guise
> A sight, that, to please a true Britisher's eyes.
> And then the Society—surely that will be
> Supported by Britons, ask Good Walter Gilbey.

In 1893 he was created a baronet, and three years later he was elected President of the Royal Agricultural Society.

His son Walter, the second baronet, inherited his tastes and owned a fine stud of racehorses that included Paper Money, who ran third to Grand Parade and Buchan in the 1919 Derby. Paper Money was by Greenback out of Epping Rose, and Sir Walter bought him at the July Sales at Newmarket for £500. It was one of his best bargains, Paper Money winning many races. At the end of his career, Sir Walter sold him as a stallion to New Zealand, where his stock prospered.

Among his other excellent horses mention should be made of Bridgewater, Race Rock and Burnside. Race Rock won the Great Ebor Handicap at York, and Burnside, highly popular with racegoers, was a frequent winner at Newmarket, Sir Walter's favourite course. The second Sir Walter was at least as picturesque a figure as his father. He died at the very end of the war, in April 1945 (the heir to the baronetcy, his grandson, Derek, was a prisoner-of-war in Germany). It was the day that the Americans reached the Elbe, but even with such stirring events to record, *The Times* found room for a long obituary of the octogenarian sportsman, with a photograph of him in his famous curly-brimmed bowler, a tribute to him as 'one of the best shots in the country', and reminiscences of how he not only loved horses but cared deeply about how their riders dressed, castigating with especial severity those who rode hatless in the Row.

A love of horses has become, indeed, traditional among the Gilbeys. Argo Gold had two excellent racehorses in Chiltern and Bertillion; once they both won on the same day at Windsor and an evening paper bore the heading 'Gold for Gold at Windsor'.

Audley Blyth ran third with Elliman in the Grand National. Geoffrey Gilbey won the Molyneux at Liverpool with Peace Pact. Ronald Gilbey raced on the Continent for some years, during which time his horses won some seventy races. It was Ronald who was the first member of the firm to visit Australia, arriving there in 1907, a youngster of twenty-one, to be asked by the firm's resident representative, Henry Collins, 'What have they sent a boy like you for?' But his keenness and youthful charm did much to establish Gilbey's sound position in Australia.

Like his cousin, and exact contemporary, Arthur Nockolds Gilbey, who was said to be one of the finest dry-fly fishermen in England, William Gilbey was more interested in catching fish than in racing horses; indeed, he bred fish. He had a hatchery at his home at Denham, where he reared trout. His most ambitious venture was an attempt to stock the Thames with salmon. Having heard that Danube salmon did not have to go down to the sea, he felt that this was the fish with which to stock the Thames, where pollution in the lower reaches was such, even then, that no salmon could get through it to spawn. He imported ova from the Danube, hatched them in his Denham hatchery, and put them in the Thames. There is no evidence of success. William's efforts were mocked at by *Punch*, with verses including the lines:

> Down beyond Barking Reach,
> Foul beyond power of speech,
> Went the six hundred!

Three members of the family have kept up the traditional Gilbey love of horses by being Masters of Foxhounds—the late Colonel Alfred Gilbey having been a Master of the Old Berkeley West Foxhounds; Rupert Gilbey, Master of the Vine; and Oliver Gilbey, Master of the Bicester; while several members of the third generation used to spend their holidays, when young, taking a whip in the various road coaches.

The spirit of old Sir Walter Gilbey has brooded over the leisure hours of his contemporaries and juniors, and he had certainly a striking personality. He had a great sense of style. T. P. O'Connor, in his obituary, said that he 'suggested' a Parisian dandy of the days after the Revolution rather than an Englishman, describing 'the body thin almost to a spectre but taut, alert: breathing vitality radiating from the whole fleshless person'. T. P. referred to 'the Quaker fashion of his buff waistcoat and nankeen trousers'. Major Vivian Nickalls refers to his 'tight-fitting strapped trousers, fawn-coloured coat, frilled shirt, top hat and monocle'. Many books of reminiscences speak of his exquisite hands.

Many stories have been told of his quickness in repartee. He rented for many years Cambridge House, which is Crown property and now a Government office. Edward VII when Prince of Wales often drove in Sir Walter's carriage: once when passing Cambridge House he asked, 'Whose house is this?' 'Yours, Sir,' was the answer.

He built himself a carriage to his own design, with the brake lever controlled from the inside, and his appearance at Ascot, driving with four grey horses and postillions, always caused a sensation. The Prince of Wales once said to him, 'Damn it, Sir Walter, not only do you match your horses, but your riders as well! How do you manage it?' Sir Walter's reply was, 'Breed 'em, Sir!' It was true enough, for the two riders were the Patmore brothers, the son of one of whom worked in the firm until his death in 1953.

The first Sir Walter Gilbey was undoubtedly the most picturesque personality among the original partners, but the others in their own fashion made their mark upon their day. Alfred Gilbey died young in 1879, but not before his home, Wooburn House, had become a centre of local life. He was a typical Victorian philanthropist, the poor man who has made money quickly, who is conscious of a debt to the community, and who devoted his leisure to 'good works'. He restored the church, enlarged the school, added to the amenities of the village green.

James Blyth, like the other early partners, was a staunch Liberal. He was to be made first a baronet and then a baron. He, too, was to be a friend of royalty, and a plan exists of a dinner he gave in May 1897 at 33, Portland Place, in honour of the Prince of Wales and the massive Prince Edward of Saxe-Weimar. Fifty-two men sat round the table: the guests were drawn chiefly from the theatrical profession and it is a tribute to their prominence that even now few of their names are unfamiliar—Tree and Irving and John Hare, Anthony Hope and Weedon Grossmith—they were all there, with the Prince's particular crony, Christopher Sykes, a shadow now of the heavy swell of the 'sixties, and nearly at the sad, stricken end of his life. The genial Henry Gold and his tall bearded brother, Charles, were among the guests. They, too, were prominent personalities. Henry Gold was High Sheriff of Berkshire in 1897. His brother, Charles, was Liberal M.P. for the Saffron Walden Division of Essex from 1895 to 1900 and was knighted in 1906.

Of the original partners, Henry Grinling alone took little interest in public affairs; concentrating upon the storage department, spending more of his time at Camden Town than in the Pantheon, he lived a little outside the close clan co-operation of the Gilbeys, the Blyths and Golds. His own home, Harrow Weald House, was very markedly the centre of his immediate family, each of his three sons making their homes near him.

Strong though the clan instinct among the Gilbeys was, it is to be noted that they achieved their prominence in spheres outside the immediate interests of their business. And close though the emotional ties between them, in spite of the constant and continued intermarriage of first and second cousins, each partner led a separate social life. Perhaps this is because they were dealing direct with agencies rather than with private customers, and consequently did not in the run of their business make as many stimulating connections as does the average wine merchant. They made no attempt to poach on the clientèle of old-established firms. It was neither in their nature nor in their interest to do so, and the average connoisseur of wine is as reluctant to change his wine merchant as his lawyer. In this respect it is pertinent to print a letter that the firm received from Mr. Gladstone.

It was not until very near the close of his life that Mr. Gladstone had any dealings with the firm as a customer, although he was personally acquainted with more than one of the partners, especially as there was a strong tradition of service to the Liberal Party among them, and he occasionally conferred with them on public matters. Because his treatment of the wine duties had given rise to malicious suggestions that he was in some way pecuniarily interested in the success of the firm, he more than once took public occasion to deny emphatically that he had any connection with the business, but, four years before his death, in the delicate health that followed his retirement from active politics—he was eighty-five—he was recommended by his doctor to drink an astringent type of wine, and having failed to obtain it elsewhere, he applied to Messrs. Gilbey, as being likely, with their extensive connections, to help him. After some little trouble they succeeded, and their services were thus acknowledged:

Hawarden, *August 27th*, 1894

Dear Sirs,

You have indeed outstripped all my requests, and I thank you very much. . . .

I may truly say that I have always regarded the proceedings of your firm with a peculiar interest. You have been, as far as I am able to form an opinion, in an eminent sense, and in a degree with which no one can compete, the openers of the wine trade.

The process has, I trust, been satisfactory to yourselves: it has certainly been one highly beneficial to the country: and (like the really great enterprise of Messrs. Cook) you stand outside and above the rank of ordinary commercial houses.

(Private)—I should myself long ago have carried to you my insignificant custom, but for my systematic disinclination to part company with those whom I have long known and dealt with.

I remain, Dear Sirs,
With much respect,
Faithfully yours,
W. E. GLADSTONE

It is not unlikely that a great many other wine drinkers felt as Mr. Gladstone did, and the partners relied for their social contacts on their more personal pursuits. But the directors of the firm must have been pleased to have this tribute in 1894 from one whose budget of 1860 they had turned to such good account.

CHAPTER IX

The Second Generation

THE distillery in Camden Town was opened in 1872, fifteen years after the firm started business, and by then a second generation was preparing to take the place of the original founding partners. Between 1880 and 1885 three of Alfred Gilbey's sons, Alfred, William Crosbie and Newman, were admitted as partners. In 1883 they were joined by Walter's son, Henry Walter, to be followed in 1890 by his brother, Arthur Nockolds. In 1885 a place was found for Henry Gold's son, Argo, and there were four schoolboys, Arthur Gold, Gibbons Grinling, Herbert and Arthur Blyth, the sons respectively of Charles Gold, Henry Grinling, James and Henry Blyth, waiting to take their places in the firm. Only one of the original partners was unrepresented by a son in this new generation—Henry Parry Gilbey, who died in 1892.

The period during which this second generation controlled the firm is unmarked by any of the vicissitudes of fortune that dramatized the firm's opening years, or by the alternating booms and slumps which forced on so many other firms, after World War I, the need of reconstruction. The 'nineties was the most prosperous decade in English history. And as regards big business—whatever it may have been in artistic coteries—it was also a placid one.

Only one major landmark stands out in the panorama of the 'nineties, and that is the conversion of the business into a limited liability company in 1893, when large sums of money had to be found to meet death duties on the estate of Henry Parry Gilbey. The tangible assets amounted to £1,280,000 and there appeared, in addition, the item of £720,000 for goodwill, making the total assets £2,000,000. In this context mention should be made of the remarkable services of A. J. Burke, who carried through the incorporation of the company and had served for over 50 years as company secretary when he died in harness in 1943 at the age of 84.

These figures are a convincing proof of the success that rewarded the energy and enterprise of the founder-partners. The omens could not have been happier. In the eighteen-nineties, a firm as soundly established as Gilbey's demanded of the directors little beyond prudence. The business ran itself, expanding normally as markets automatically increased.

To such an extent did markets increase that by 1914 the premises at Camden Town were covering a floor area of 20 acres, of which the gin distillery occupied only a part. Each part was devoted to its own special function, packing, bottling, labelling; the storage of wines and spirits, the storage of light wines; the duty-paid, the bottle and bonded warehouses, capable of storing 800,000 gallons. The volume of business had become so great that the London and North Western Railway constructed a whole network of rails to reach the export department. Every day a train known as 'Gilbey's Special' left for the London Docks.

Adjoining the bonded and duty-paid warehouses and the distillery by now was the bottle warehouse, put up in 1894, one of the first ferro-concrete buildings in London, with immensely thick walls which, it was light-heartedly alleged in the firm, were reinforced with old bedsteads and cast-off bicycle frames. Originally intended for empty bottles and cases, it soon included the engineers' shops, in which two powerful steam engines throbbed all day; the carpenters' department, where saws sliced wood for packing cases; and, on the roof, tons of timber being seasoned for the same job.

The bottle warehouse was the creation (as were some of the new buildings at Loudenne) of a remarkable character, William Hucks, engaged originally as the firm's first gin distiller, but so much a man of parts that he was soon its chief engineer and architect. But this is to make him sound as professional in manner as he was skilful—and professional Grandfather Hucks was not. He prepared no plans; built as he went along; and refused to submit estimates, saying, 'It'll cost what it'll cost'—which, indeed, it did.

By now the export trade represented a large part of the firm's turnover. There were agencies in every country and in most big foreign cities. The firm had been one of the first, if not actually the first, to ship wine in bottle to the Far East, and so brisk was the demand for what was called in those days 'Spanish port' that many imitations appeared upon the market. These imitations came from Hamburg, and legal action resulted in the destruction of a huge consignment of labels which had been printed in flagrant imitation of the Gilbey style. Later, when a treaty between Portugal and Great Britain established that only wine produced in Portugal could be described as Port this brand was renamed 'Spanish Red Wine'. Under its new label it continued to prove very popular.

To deal with this overseas trade, specially trained young men who had to be expert linguists were sent out as commercial envoys. The first of them was F. G. Collins, who visited the Far East in 1884, and a record such as this should not leave unmentioned the excellent services that were rendered by William Dennis, the brothers Douglas, William Bruce and Charles Preston, and Captain Montague Polley. Each of these envoys was given a separate territory, for it was soon realized that periodic visits were not sufficient, and resident representatives were essential, so that local publicity could be prepared and local conditions appreciated at the Pantheon.

The country is happy which has no history, and that is pre-eminently true of the House of Gilbey during this second quarter of its history. Business was good and the clan spirit, the very real affection that united the several families, prevented any of those internal dissensions that so often disrupt an otherwise fortunately placed undertaking. There were no cantankerous shareholders to spread ill-will. Such disagreements on policy as arose from time to time were settled in amicable discussion. There were no angry resignations. The firm's difficulties have in fact all come from outside, in particular from the activities of successive Chancellors of the Exchequer in exacting tribute from the wine trade.

Gilbey's difficulties have been since early days those of the wine trade as a whole; in 1906 a Liberal Government, very conscious of strong Nonconformist support, was returned to the House of Commons with a large majority. Reform of the licensed trade had been one of the planks in its election platform, and in 1908 Asquith introduced his Licensing Bill, which proposed, among other things, to impose a 'time limit', after which liquor licences should have no right to renewal. Great indignation was aroused, not among licence holders but with the general public; popular demonstrations against the Bill culminated in the Peckham by-election which resulted in the return of the Conservative candidate by a majority of over 2,000: a reversal of public opinion which was accepted, tacitly or openly, by all parties as a public condemnation of the Bill.

The Bill's subsequent rejection in the House of Lords provided, however, only a brief armistice, for the Lords' support of 'the right to get drunk' infuriated the Nonconformists, who 'rallied more and more behind Lloyd George', as G. D. H. Cole has recorded, 'in readiness to hit back when the chance came'. So that when, in 1909, Lloyd George, as Chancellor of the Exchequer, introduced his famous budget which led to the 'Peers *v.* People' election of 1910, the radical wing of the Liberal Party triumphed, and with its triumph came the eclipse of the power of the upper house. This Lloyd George budget of 1909 raised the duty on spirits from 11*s.* to 14*s.* 9*d.* per proof gallon, and increased very heavily the duties in respect of all classes of liquor licences. Numerous and intricate changes were also made in the details affecting the various types of licence.

In the ensuing difficult negotiations between the Government and the licensed trade, the House played a responsible part.

Henry Grinling, who had been one of the representatives of the licensed trade, was Chairman of the Royal Commission on the Liquor Licensing Laws. James Blyth, Arthur N. Gilbey (President of the National Federation of Off-licence Holders' Associations) and Argo Gold (controlling the sales organization of the House) all fought hard for the rights of the trade; with Argo Gold, who was also in charge of the Advice Bureau which the House had set up for its retailers, organizing in 1910 a service which was justly described as unique in the licensed trade. Under this scheme every retailer on the books was invited to complete a form stating the licences then held by him and the licences which he would hold under the new conditions. The complicated adjustments of licence duty provided by the new Act were calculated and scheduled, and each retailer received, within a few days of sending in his form, a table showing the exact sums with which he would be charged. Thousands of forms were dealt with, and this vast task was completed within nine weeks of its inception. It may be noted that the Advice Bureau still remains in operation, with its facilities available to all holders of liquor licences of any kind.

In the same year a codifying Act, known as the Licensing (Consolidation) Act, 1910, was passed, and the Bureau had to convey the necessary explanations of the new law affecting Justices' Licences: the Bureau's services were again required in 1911, when the Finance Act of that year made some additional changes in the law affecting the licensed trade. Three years later the outbreak of war further complicated the working of the licensing laws.

These many problems did not, however, prevent the firm from expanding its business and developing its own special lines. Gilbey's were by now one of the largest port shippers in the country. Although they were in a position to supply vintage port to those very many of their customers who preferred it, they had, in keeping with their tradition of supplying a medium-priced wine for the family table, specialized in wood ports. Realizing the need of a port at a moderate price and of low astringency, specially suited to the needs of invalids and convalescents, that would at the same time be palatable to those fortunate enough to need no medicine, they promoted as

'Invalid Port' in 1912 a wine that had figured unobtrusively on their list for thirty years. They introduced it to the public with the famous black-and-white 'arrow' poster: on the label appeared a perfect if unconsciously used example of an elegiac line, 'Bottled in brilliant condition but care must be used in decanting'.

This campaign to launch 'Invalid Port', though no one quite realized it at the time, came to be recognized later as a key date in the history of the firm. It was the first occasion on which Gilbey's had backed a proprietary brand with a big publicity campaign, and it had an unexpected consequence: it killed the system of appointing special agents with exclusive rights to a territory. There was clearly no point in offering a branded commodity to the general public if individual members of that public could not obtain the advertised commodity at the particular store they patronized. Gilbey's products, from now on, had to be universally 'obtainable'. It was the first stage in the global development that was the characteristic feature of the between-wars and post-second-war periods.

Gilbey's Offices, Haymarket, Edinburgh

Whisky Bottling Lines, Haymarket, Edinburgh

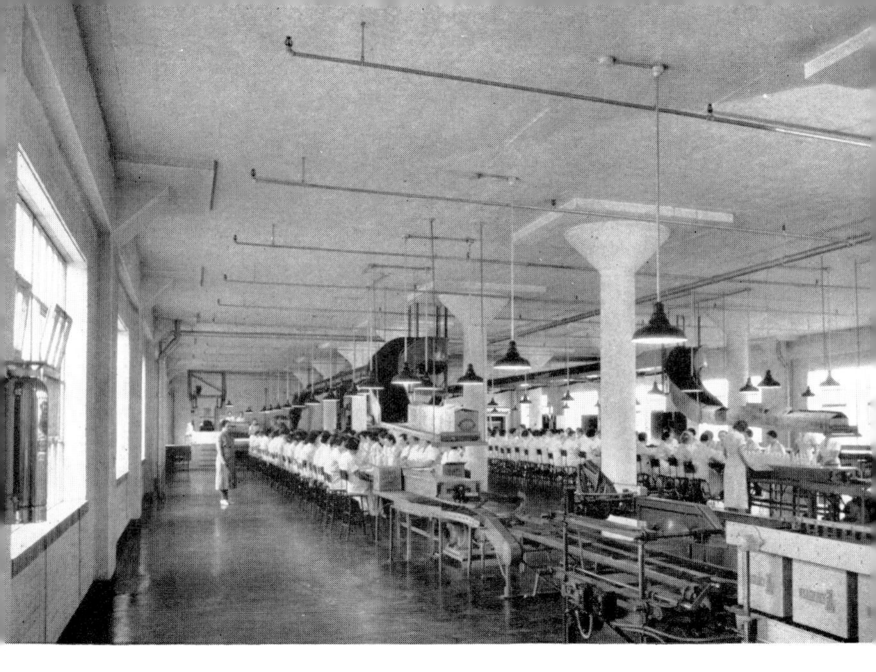

Gin Bottling Lines, Cincinnati, U.S.A.

Gin Stills, Cincinnati, U.S.A.

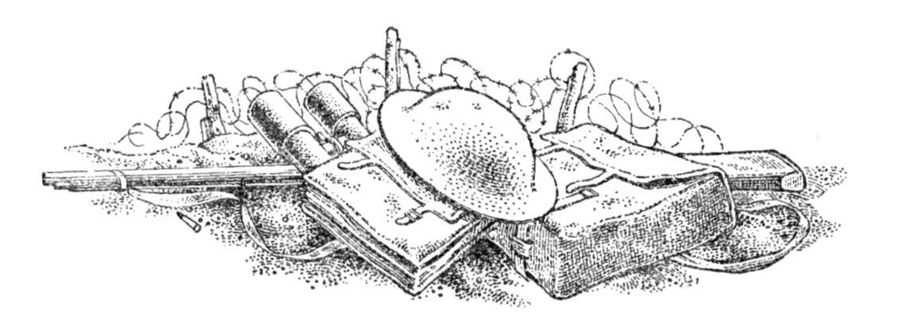

CHAPTER X

The Third Generation

THE second generation had a relatively easy task, by the standards of difficulty of the atom age. Even World War I seems, in retrospect, to have presented the partners with few serious problems. It is true that many members of the staff, as of the Board, joined the armed forces, and there had to be re-allocations of duties. There were also shortages and restrictions. The distillation of spirits was stopped entirely, the firm's distilleries were commandeered to produce acetone for shells and yeast for bread, while the engineering department was engaged in the production of 13-lb. shells; large consignments of West Indian rum were requisitioned for the troops overseas; and rationing orders limited the supplier of wines and spirits to a percentage, only, of his previous orders, so that many small firms found themselves crippled by shortage of supplies and of staff, and by the limited drawings allowed from bond.

But Gilbey's was by now so large a firm, its resources and reserves so vast, that it could afford to accept as no more than an inconvenience restrictions and controls that drove many of their less fortunate rivals out of business. In 1860 the partners had had to think very quickly when Gladstone's budget destroyed the market for Cape wines. Then, they had had all their eggs, such as they were, in a single basket. By 1914 there were many baskets. They were able to maintain a steady supply of gin through the vast quantities of Cape spirit, for which they owned the appropriate rectifying plant. Even the shipping of port continued, though it presented many problems, of which the adventures of a sailing vessel, the *Rio Mondego*, provide a typical example. She had been chartered to ship a thousand pipes from Oporto. A German submarine intercepted her and forced the crew to take to boats; but its efforts to torpedo the ship proved unavailing as her cargo kept her afloat. A British destroyer intervened, forced the submarine to dive, rescued the crew and towed the ship to Swansea, where salvage operations started. Two-thirds of the cargo was discovered to be sound. Gilbey's wanted to get their hands on it at once, but much money was involved and the litigation was so prolonged that the wine was not freed till the war was over.

Situations of that kind provided a succession of day-to-day problems at the Pantheon, but the end of the war found the firm ready to expand with the coming of peace.

For the third generation, however, the generation that put off its uniform in 1919, the journey was to prove less smooth.

On the second anniversary of the Armistice, two hundred and fifty ex-service members of the staff were paraded in the Pantheon to honour the unveiling of a memorial tablet designed by Sir Aston Webb. The list of those who had worn uniform in the war made an impressive record. Fifty-six sons and grandsons of the original partners and over three hundred members of the staff had seen active service. Two sons of directors, four grandsons of original partners, and thirty-seven members of the staff had lost their lives. The parade was inspected by General Sir George Higginson, a veteran of the Crimean War, where the original partners had heard gunfire.

Lord Peel, representing the War Office, made one of the chief speeches.

> It is well [he said], now that we stand on safe ground and look back over the great issues of the war, that we should realize

frankly and truthfully how tremendous were the risks we ran, and in many cases how narrow the margin by which we may have escaped disaster. Let us take this to heart. Let us not imitate our forefathers after the Napoleonic Wars, who ceased to interest themselves in military matters. I am not talking of the Army, I am talking of the people who ceased to interest themselves in military affairs, and the result was the terrible mistakes which cost us so many good lives in the Crimea, when we at last awoke. I am asking you gentlemen today not to forget this lesson.

Colonel Gilbey has told you that we are reconstructing the Army upon a new basis, upon a voluntary basis. It was very easy to cry out for the abolition of conscription—it was easy to say 'Let us go back to the old voluntary basis'—but it is not everyone who realizes the tremendous responsibilities that are cast, not on the Government or the Army, but upon the people of this country to respond to the needs of that voluntary basis. We are trying to reconstruct our Territorial Army, and for that we want all the help that you can give us. We know that, as is natural, there is much war weariness; we know that there are many men who, having fought through this war, feel that they do not want to touch military matters or look upon a military weapon again.

The great new Territorial Citizen Army which is being constructed is to be something like two and a half times the size of the small Regular Army. It is to be constructed as a complete Army, and is to stand behind that small Regular Army upon which we must rely, and which is to be for the future the source of expansion for the great National Army if the time should come. To build that up we want the experience and the discipline and the service of the men who have themselves served in the war, but we want also, coming after them and backing them up, those young men who are growing into manhood—those young men who have not seen the stress and strain of war, but who, when they come to their years of strength, will recognize that it is their obligation to those who have fought for them and fallen for them themselves to become protectors of their country, which their predecessors have maintained for them.

Those words have for us today the melancholy significance that attaches to an unheeded warning. But it is at the same time pertinent to recall that the House of Gilbey did not ignore the lessons of the past.

This great business [Lord Peel went on to say] is going to do its best to support the movement. Colonel Gilbey has permitted

> me to say what the firm will do, and what assistance it will give the young men who join the Territorial Army. In addition to the other holiday they may have—they will have of course to attend camp and do their drills—they will have a full fortnight's extra holiday on full pay. I said to Colonel Gilbey, 'I think that is a very generous and a very patriotic offer.' He said to me, 'We merely think that is our duty.' But may I be permitted to express my opinion, which is that it is a generous and patriotic offer to my official mind and perhaps I may say that it is a more generous offer than the Government themselves are giving to their own employees.

A high proportion of Gilbey's younger men availed themselves of this offer.

The ceremony was planned as a tribute to the firm's war record, but now, in retrospect, we can see it as the start of a new chapter, the entrance of the third generation. And it was prophetic that a veteran of the Crimean War should have been chosen to inspect the parade, for there was to prove a close parallel between the experiences of the original partners and of the post-war generation, just as twenty-five years later there was to be a second parallel with those of the fourth generation who returned in 1945 from its tanks and airfields to office desks.

In 1857 Walter and Alfred Gilbey and Henry Grinling had returned from the Crimea, their wits sharpened and their resistance toughened by their experiences overseas, ready to adjust themselves to sudden change, to take advantage of good fortune and to sidestep bad; it was in very much the same spirit and with the background of similar experience that the third generation returned to the Pantheon in 1919.

There were five of them in all. Four of them—Walter Gilbey's grandson, Sebastian, the son of Arthur, two of Alfred Gilbey's grandsons, Ronald and Gordon, and Charles Gold's grandson, Geoffrey, the son of Arthur—had already spent some months in the firm before the war. By August 1914 five of them had enlisted. Geoffrey Gold, one of the few civilians holding a flying licence—he was number 6—was immediately posted to the Royal Flying Corps and flew over the lines in France, in a ramshackle kite of a machine armed only with a rifle. During the war two others of the third generation reached military age, Henry Gold's grandson, Alec, the son of Argo, and Henry Grinling's grandson, Antony, who was awarded the M.C.

All six of them were back in the Pantheon in 1919, to be joined a little later by Arthur Blyth's son, Derek.

They had come from the same tense atmosphere of war as the original founders of the business, yet their preliminary peace-time training could not have been more different. When Henry Gilbey drove his coach from Bishop's Stortford, half a dozen public schools existed, but not 'the public-school system' as it is understood today, for Arnold had not yet been appointed to Rugby, nor was there yet the middle-class demand for the kind of school that would give boys the accent and manners of those educated at the seven schools that were formally to be recognized in the Act of 1870 as 'public schools'—Eton, Harrow, Winchester, Shrewsbury, Charterhouse, Westminster and Rugby. Marlborough, Cheltenham and Haileybury had not yet been founded; Sherborne, Tonbridge, Uppingham were local grammar schools with twenty to thirty day-boys. There was no compulsory education, no school-leaving age. The Gilbeys, the Golds, the Blyths, the Grinlings began to earn their living as soon as they reached their teens. Their grandsons, however, were all expensively educated, at Eton or Harrow or, in the case of the Catholic branch, at Ampleforth or Beaumont. During the intervening years the public-school system had flowered from a matter of six to sixty institutions to meet the needs, and to accommodate the growth, of families like the House of Gilbey.

The fact that the third generation were educated at establishments that old Henry Gilbey would have regarded as the particular preserve of the aristocracy and landed gentry did not by any means introduce into the Pantheon a superior, stand-offish atmosphere. On the contrary it was in the late Victorian and early Edwardian periods that 'starchiness' was to be encountered there. Most of us who were born in the 'nineties can remember seeing our fathers start off each morning for their city offices in high silk hats. The London editor of the *Manchester Guardian*, James Bone, recalled on retiring from the paper in 1945 that when he had joined the staff in 1901 he was the only member without a silk hat. 'Now,' he said, 'I am the only member of the staff with one.' And an Australian merchant who for many years had had a substantial account with the firm was fond of recounting his experience in the 'nineties, when in the course of a visit to London he called at the Pantheon. He was expansively and expensively entertained by the export manager, T. A. Sleap, who after lunch sought out the partner in charge of the export department, to effect an introduction with so important a customer. The partner in question, looking down the office, was shocked to see at its far end a large red-faced man in a ready-made lounge suit and bowler hat. 'What!' he exclaimed. 'That man there in a bowler hat? I can't see anyone like that.' Nor could the dimensions of the colonial visitor's account persuade him to change his mind.

No such incident could take place today in Oval Road.

Nineteen-twenty, the year of the War Memorial unveiling at the Pantheon, was one of great industrial unrest. The previous year had seen a succession of major strikes, and the threat of a general strike was growing. It nearly came in the late spring of 1921, and several speeches at the ceremony referred to 'the torn and riven fabric of our national unity'. 'At every street corner at the weekend,' Lord Burnham said, 'there will be men who are professors of sedition preaching the class war.' But in actual fact it was not from this source that the problems of the third generation were to come.

In the early nineteen-twenties the firm profited from the immediate and inevitable post-war boom. Although the duty on whisky was raised from the 1914 figure of 14*s.* 9*d.* per proof gallon to 72*s.* 6*d.*, on ports and sherries from 3*s.* to 6*s.*, and on table wines from 1*s.* 3*d.* to 2*s.* 6*d.* a gallon, the demand for wine and spirits during those first years was phenomenal. But the firm recognized that such easy markets would not long remain. They were on their guard for danger signs. One of the first came from the other side of the world where, owing to its lower rate of duty, Australian-made gin had become such a dangerous rival that in 1927 Geoffrey and Alec Gold toured the country to examine conditions on the spot. As a result of their report an establishment was set up for bottling in Melbourne London-made gin of high strength, shipped in drums. This, however, only proved a temporary expedient and in 1934 it was decided to produce gin in Australia on the London formula. In 1927 the total investment in Australia was £25,000; today it stands at one million Australian pounds.

In Canada, too, local competition soon forced the house to install a distillery in Toronto. As the first partners had travelled over Europe, forming direct relations with wine-growers and shippers, so the third generation travelled throughout the Empire making the business global, enlarging the number of their agencies, setting up distilleries in the New World.

At first, gin only was distilled in Australia, but later a local whisky was produced. Both these distilleries were planned by Crosbie Hucks; it has already been recorded that his grandfather started the London distillery, his father later managed it. His grandmother was Julia, sister of the original founders, whose great grand-nephew he thus is. At the time of writing Crosbie Hucks is President of the Federal Wine and Spirit Association of Australia.

It may here be noted that the clan spirit is not only confined to the partners in the firm; there are other constant names upon the payroll. The most notable example, along with that of the three generations of Huckses, is that of the Carvers. The firm's present accountant, J. H. Carver, succeeded his father, A. L. Carver, in the position, and he had succeeded *his* father, A. G. Carver, who had joined Gilbey's in 1870. A. G. Carver was a lively, sociable man in the London of the eighteen-seventies and later; a cello player and possessor of an agreeable tenor voice; and one of the first to ride a penny-farthing bicycle. He was a personal friend of the first directors, and was trustee of the estates of Henry Parry Gilbey and the first Sir Walter. He retired in 1930, after sixty years' service. Reference has already been made in the previous chapter to the brothers Douglas and to Frederick Collins, who were among the first representatives of the firm abroad. Charles Douglas's son Robert is now Sales Manager in Canada, while the market for gin that Frederick Collins built up in Australia was handled after his death, first by his brother Henry and later by his nephew Edmund, one of the finest salesmen the firm ever had.

This sense of continuity and family tradition is, no doubt, in large part responsible for the long periods of service among the staff. In Scotland between 1859 and 1952 there were only three managers. In 1945 there were nine men upon the register who had worked at the Pantheon fifty years before.

CHAPTER XI

Fashions in Wines and Spirits between the Wars

THE exploitation of these new markets for gin and whisky did not result in any neglect of the Médoc wines on which the firm's fortunes had so soon after its foundation come to be based, and in August 1919 Gordon Gilbey went down to Bordeaux to see what effect five years of war had had on Château Loudenne.

He set out in a mood of understandable apprehension. Since 1914, with German submarines having been active in the Channel and in the Atlantic, the shipping of wine from France had presented many difficulties, some of them insuperable; there had been a great labour shortage; the two managers, Georges Bayle and Camille Gombeau, had been mobilized, and though their wives had carried on in their absence with Annamite labourers helping in the vineyards, it was doubtful whether it had been possible to do much more than keep the machine ticking over. And indeed Gordon Gilbey was to find much there to disquiet him. The rapid rise in the cost of living in France had hit the peasant hard.

With the franc at seventy to the pound, the standard rate of six francs a day for a man and two and a half for a woman was pitifully low. Work in the vineyards was, in fact, one of the worst-paid forms of employment in the country. Gordon Gilbey soon realized the position and raised the daily wages; and gave a dance upon the terrace as an earnest indication that new conditions would produce a new relationship between employer and employed. From this time on, he made the care and welfare of Château Loudenne his special province, and its prosperity between the wars was in the main due to him.

Shortage of labour was a constant problem, as in all the great wine-growing countries and, indeed, in agriculture everywhere, for the young men and women of the new generation preferred to work in towns: moreover, the demand for claret in England was diminishing owing to its high cost. In 1925, 1,036 hogsheads were produced, but several vineyards were later allowed to go out of cultivation. In 1929, 608 hogsheads were produced, and in 1934, 653, but by 1936 production had been considerably reduced. Even so, the Château's value as a depot was undiminished, and its ownership gave Gilbey's a status in the Bordeaux wine trade that no other English house possessed.

Every great war produces changes in the social structure of a country; changes that inevitably affect its drinking habits. There is here a problem for the wine merchant, who cannot create a change in fashion as can a dress designer, and who must have consequently the most sensitive of antennae to recognize a change when it is on its way, so that he can discriminate between a passing whim and a genuine change of taste. To those of us who had no adult life before 1914, it seems in retrospect that those twenty years between the wars were marked by a succession of changes in the drinking habits of the country.

During World War I, the poor quality of beer at home and a shortage of spirits, together with many a young subaltern's experience of the *estaminets* of France, or of wines drunk in the Army of Occupation in Cologne, made many English people turn to wine, and the taste once acquired was maintained, though there was a constant change in the kinds of wine that were being drunk. The various Chancellors of the Exchequer had a good deal to do with this. The tax on champagne, for instance, was so high that people began to wonder whether it was 'all that good'. Its merits were decried and it went out of favour. And it may be, too, that French wine-growers and middlemen, after the lean wartime years, were too eager to market wines, especially abroad, regardless of their quality. It was not till the middle 'thirties that the two great vintage years of 1926 and 1928 restored champagne to the proud and rightful position that it had held in the days of Swithin Forsyte.

There was also a reaction against both burgundy and vintage port—a reaction that appeared to coincide, curiously enough, with the formation early in the nineteen-thirties of the Wine and Food Society. The last thing that the founders of that excellent organization would have wished was to disparage two such noble wines; but the publicity that accrued to wine in general, as a result of its foundation, made a great number of people anxious to appear knowledgeable about wine; claret, with its sixty-one châteaux in five growths, gives plenty of scope for winemanship. Connoisseurship in claret is simplified by château-bottling, and by the more accurate and detailed classification of châteaux, vineyards and districts. You can pick up a wine list and know where you are. There is no such certainty in burgundy. When the Saintsbury Club was entertained in Paris in 1938 by the Club des Cents, the great wine served at the summit of the evening, after a Mouton-Rothschild 1924, was Beaune 1928, *tout court*. Now, 'Beaune 1928' in an English country inn might mean anything; whereas a château-bottled Talbot 1929, unless it had been subjected to barbarous treatment and exposed to the extremities of heat and cold, could be regarded as guaranteed.

It is not, perhaps, surprising that there should have been a reaction against burgundy at a time when people with inexperienced palates were anxious to appear connoisseurs, but it is at a first glance surprising that there should have been a simultaneous reaction against vintage port, a subject on which Englishmen for two hundred years and more—ever since the Methuen Treaty of 1703 with Portugal—have prided themselves on being knowledgeable. To tell one shipper's wine from another is the work of an expert, but the varied wines produced and shipped, and the difference between the wines of one year and those of another, provide ample scope for the student. Moreover, port has this advantage—that it is much easier to taste one wine against another when you have not to drink at a single sitting the entire bottle you have decanted.

The reaction against vintage port in the nineteen-thirties may possibly be the corollary to a corollary. Psychoanalysts are continually informing us that we give false reasons for our actions without knowing that we are doing it, in order to conceal our real reasons from ourselves. Is it too fanciful to suggest that the neophyte of wine, having expressed a preference for claret, actually because it was easier to appraise, but in his declared opinion because it was more pure, felt himself bound for the same reason to distrust a wine that had been fortified? Or was it a further instalment of the reaction against port for after dinner that had first set in, as recorded in Chapter V, in Queen Victoria's times, with the coming of tobacco to the dining-room? Then, in the robust days of Edward, Prince of Wales, the gentlemen had continued to sit after dinner, once the ladies had withdrawn, but drinking, often, instead of port, brandy—as better able to withstand the rich fumes of smouldering Havana. Now, in the days of another Edward, Prince of Wales—the Prince Charming who had served in the trenches with the Welsh Guards—many a gently-born household no longer found its men sitting in the dining-room after dinner at all, over whatever drink: how can a man sit over his wine when mute wifely pleas for a hand with the washing-up are being wafted by thought transference from the kitchen? And habits learned in the home persisted in the clubs: many will recall the Garrick Club selling at auction, during World War II, the port with which it was now overstocked, because of the changing habits of members, in order to buy the greater amount of table wine now being asked for. Whatever the reason, it is an undoubted fact that wine merchants found themselves in the mid-'thirties unable to dispose of the excellent '27 vintage that they had imported in large quantities, and the same was true of other later great wines. For those who survived World War II, it is extremely lucky that this was so. Otherwise, there would not be so much good port in the country still.

There was also, and not unnaturally, in the later nineteen-twenties, a vogue for German wines. During the war they had been unobtainable, and for a time after the war there was a feeling that it was unpatriotic to drink German wines. That feeling did not last for long, and the very fact that they had been long deprived of them made the English appreciate more fully, when they finally came to savour them, the delicate flavour of Moselle and the superb bouquets of the great estate-bottled Hocks. The hot summer of 1921 gave German wines a unique opportunity to recover their popularity.

There were other changes for which, again, the Treasury was responsible. In 1927 Mr. Baldwin's Chancellor of the Exchequer, Mr. Winston Churchill, though he increased the wine duties, allowed an imperial preference on Empire wines. In this way he reversed Gladstone's policy. The preference was intended to aid the Australian dessert wines and a certain demand grew up for sweet red and white types that were known by the generic name of 'Austral'. This happened in a boom period, and though there was a certain demand for these wines, they were drunk for the most part, at first, in modest homes. But after the economic crisis of September 1931, when Britain was forced off the gold standard and it became both necessary to economize and patriotic to 'buy British', a more careful attention was paid to Empire wines.

South African wines in particular came into favour. The Wine and Food Society gave a very successful South African dinner at which fifteen different kinds of sparkling wine were shown, all from the Cape. The wheel had, in fact, come full circle. The Gilbeys had founded a business to sell Cape wines to a new class of wine-drinker who could not afford French or German wines. Seventy-five years later, they were doing precisely the same thing: a class that could not afford French and German wines was asking them to provide sound, cheap, wholesome wines from the Cape. And now, in the firm's centenary year, there are excellent Cape wines in its list, well-known and welcome to all classes of wine-drinker and to every income group.

But far more important than the various changes that were enforced by the raising and lowering of customs' duties was the revolution in social and drinking habits that followed the introduction of the cocktail party. It is hard to give an exact date for the beginning of the cocktail party. The idea came, presumably, from America. By 1927 it was already established in London. There are indications that during 1925 it was finding itself. Guests were tending to drop in for a cocktail at six, rather than for 'a dish of tea' at half-past four; but in 1924 it was relatively unknown. The present writer recalls how, in April 1924, he discussed with C. R. W. Nevinson, the painter, and his wife, the difficulty of finding anything to do in London in the winter between tea and dinner. The Nevinsons decided that it might be a good time at which to give a party and sent out an announcement that they were emerging from their winter retirement and would be at home on the last Saturday in April between five and seven. Questioned, years afterwards, they were vague as to the number of invitations they sent out; but some thirty glasses were arranged beside a large earthenware jug containing a yellow, coolish but not cold mixture, in which rum was the chief ingredient. Only two guests arrived. The Londoners of the Nevinsons' acquaintance—and the Nevinsons touched life at very many points—were puzzled by the novelty of the invitation. And Londoners tend socially to avoid what puzzles them.

Remembering the experience of the Nevinsons, this writer, wishing to give a cocktail party in October 1925, took the precaution of inviting his friends to tea at half-past four and not starting to serve cocktails until half-past five. He served a rum swizzle, mixed by a New York friend. It was sweet, cold and strong, and a distinguished woman novelist who, because it was cold and sweet, mistook it for a kind of sherbet, failed to achieve her subsequent engagement for dinner. Within a mere eighteen months the cocktail party was an established form of entertainment. For a quarter of a century it retained its popularity, though it yielded to some extent, after World War II, to the sherry party and, more recently still, to the party at which simple table wine is drunk. But the cocktail party still survives, growing more elaborate as time has passed; for substantial food is now provided, and hostesses have come to realize that unless they specifically state 6 p.m–8 p.m. on their invitation, or unless, in winter time, they start opening windows and stop serving drinks, they must be prepared to have at least a quarter of their guests stay on to supper.

As the cocktail party vogue increased, so, inevitably, did the demand for Gilbey's gin. For gin is the basis of all the most popular cocktails, though 'Odds-On', the one ready-mixed cocktail marketed at home by Gilbey's (there is a ready-mixed Martini sold abroad) * is a true wine cocktail, as the label states, and is very popular. But 'Odds-On', launched in the nineteen-thirties and still of universal importance, is an exception to prove a rule. For those English people who mix their own cocktails, gin is the main ingredient; even in days when currency restrictions did not prohibit the import of rye and Bourbon whisky, such mixed drinks as are based on them—Manhattans and Old Fashioneds, for instance—were little known in England. Rum cocktails need a swizzle stick and more ingredients and more skill in mixing than the average hostess can supply. There have been changes in the actual types of cocktail that have been drunk; the Bronx is less popular than it was and Martinis have grown drier—thanks, no doubt, to the influence of visiting Americans. Gilbey's have issued an amusing illustrated folder in the shape of a gin bottle, tabulating the various ingredients required for a Bronx, a Gimlet, a Martini and other classics. The quatrain commemorating the White Lady runs:

> Where ties are white and women wear
> As little as they frankly dare
> White ladies are in great demand
> (But in a glass you understand).

Fortunately, as has been stated already, one of the chief characteristics of the House of Gilbey has been its readiness to accept and welcome change. The new demand for gin, as a basis for cocktails, found the firm already ahead, rather than abreast, of fashion, for it had begun to distil gin in London as long ago as 1872—which is undoubtedly the last thing that Walter and Alfred Gilbey would have considered possible, or indeed desirable, when they put up their first sign in Berwick Street.

* The very name of this cocktail is derived from its principal ingredients, by way of a tortuous pun. It was suggested that because it contained mainly the juice of the grape—wine and brandy—it should be called 'Bacchus'. Bacchus suggested 'backers', and 'backers' to a board of directors many of whom had an equestrian turn of mind suggested the racecourse, and 'odds on'.

In those days gin was looked at askance, and few forms of beverage have been raised to favour more triumphantly during the last fifty years. Gin once had a thoroughly bad reputation. Hazlitt was upbraided for his addiction to it; it was with gin that Hogarth's drabs were sodden: one of Trollope's characters was horrified when her father, for reasons of economy, adopted it; and Saintsbury writing as late as 1920 admits to having been always sorry for gin, 'that humble and much reviled liquid which is the most specially English of all spirits'.

And yet it was only its low purchase price that gave gin this unfortunate reputation. It was cheap and, because it was cheap, it was taken in excess by poor people, who could afford nothing else, and yet, as Saintsbury went on to say, 'it was always the most wholesome of its class and a real specific for some kinds of disease.' It has diuretic properties and is excellent as an anti-diabetic.

Its discovery is attributed to a Dutch chemist, Professor Sylvius of Leyden, who died in 1672. It was first made at Schiedam in Holland from rye and it was called Geneva from the French *genièvre* because it was flavoured with juniper. At first it was sold only in apothecaries' shops, which confirms that it had a medical origin, and so popular a medicine did it prove that many apothecaries established distilleries.

It was later, however, that gin reached London. During the Stuart period the distillation and consumption of spirits in England was small. But on the accession of William and Mary, when restrictive taxes were placed on brandy as part of a tariff war against the French, permission was given to distil and retail spirits from English-grown corn. Alexander Blunt, a distiller, in a poem dated 1729, attributes to William of Orange the introduction of Geneva into England and states that William drank it. Its popularity at Court no doubt encouraged London distillers to provide a gin of their own.

The type which they eventually evolved and which is known today as London Gin is very different in taste from the original Geneva. It is produced by distilling in a pot-still highly rectified spirits together with various botanicals. Juniper berry and coriander seed are common to all brands of London Gin and give it its basic flavour. The additional botanicals which give to

New Packages by Milner Gray, R.D.I., F.S.I.A.

Left: Packages before re-styling

Gilbey's Head Office, London. Architect—Serge Chermayeff

Entrance Lobby

each separate brand its final and distinctive flavour are kept a carefully guarded secret by each distiller.

Today the name 'London Gin' refers to a type of gin rather than a place of origin, unlike 'Plymouth Gin' (which is still a geographical as well as a descriptive name), since the pressure of customs duties has forced London distillers to manufacture their gin in countries to which they used to ship it.

From 1690 onwards, London Gin was so cheap in England that it was within everyone's reach and it was even given to workpeople as part of their wages. All sorts of shops sold gin and advertisements were displayed reading—'Drunk for one penny, dead drunk for two, and clean straw provided free', so that customers could sleep off its effects. To check the spread of drunkenness, licence duties of £15 a year and revenue duties of 20*s*. a gallon were imposed in 1736, but this only led to evasion and smuggling, so that in 1743 the policy was modified and control exercised by a combination of revenue duties and the licensing of retailers under the control of the magistrates, a policy that continues to this day.

Gin remained cheap until 1914, when the price was half-a-crown a bottle, and it is only of comparatively recent years, with the invention of the cocktail, that it has become a drink for all classes.

Today gin needs no defence. It is the basis of the majority of cocktails and is an essential ingredient in the best long summer drinks—gin and tonic, gin and ginger beer, and the Tom Collins.

CHAPTER XII

Gilbey's Gin Invades the U.S.A.

A FURTHER demand for gin was supplied at the close of 1933 by the end of Prohibition in the United States. It was a change that very obviously offered immense opportunities for any English firm ready to take advantage of it. And it was in keeping with their traditions that Gilbey's did.

During Prohibition many bottles of London Gin bearing the Gilbey's label had appeared on the speakeasy market, whose contents would not always by any means have satisfied the laboratories in Camden Town. The Prohibition era is, indeed, an amusing footnote in the Gilbey saga. Gilbey labels kept arriving in London from the United States with the query, 'Are they genuine?' The copying of labels in the United States was so widespread that Gilbey's had to set up a special service to identify them. Often, only the printer could tell by the watermark if they were genuine. One ingenious racketeer bottled imitation Gilbey's gin in elaborately decorated cans, stating that no others were genuine.

The principal bases of supply were Vancouver, which worked the West Coast; Nassau, which supplied Florida and the South East; and St. Pierre de Miquelon, where large warehouses sprang up as a base for supply of the East Coast.

Dealers from these towns visited the Pantheon in person with vast sums in cash and particular requirements but were understandably vague as to the final destination of their orders. Some wanted their cases made up of lots of six bottles each, in hessian bags; others asked for wire handles. In the late nineteen-twenties and early nineteen-thirties the export warehouse was filled with rows of women sewing hessian bags to complete these orders. At that time Scotch for export was 40*s.* per case f.o.b. and gin 22*s.*, cash paid in advance, no advertising allowance. Shipment was either to Hamburg or Antwerp, to avert suspicion, and there the bootleggers took over. At St. Pierre, the wooden cases were hacked open and discarded (causing a serious disposal problem) and the bags and bottles were loaded in shallow-draught vessels which dumped their cargoes in shallow water, to be collected later by land-based operators. To protect the consumer from spurious products, a square gin bottle was produced; it was sand-blasted on three sides, with the label printed on both sides and visible through the one clear side. This was very difficult and costly to imitate—and is still used for Gilbey's U.S.A. gin. A sufficient proportion of sound alcohol had found its way into the speakeasies for Gilbey's reputation to stand high. After repeal of Prohibition it was to stand still higher, Gilbey's having formed a new company, W. & A. Gilbey Ltd. of Delaware, in partnership with National Distillers Products Corporation.

The story of National Distillers represents one of the freak case histories of modern American industry. Founded in 1902 to distil whisky and other beverage spirits, it had been, before the passage of the Eighteenth Amendment, a highly prosperous concern. Prohibition flung it out of operation. Attempts to shift into other forms of activity, such as the production of industrial alcohol and the processing of food products (under the name of the U.S. Food Products Corporation), were unsuccessful, and in 1922 the creditors called in the firm of Sanderson and Porter to salvage what they could out of the wreck. It is to the enterprise and foresight of Seton Porter that the Corporation owes its present prominence. Instead of liquidating such assets as remained he recommended that the company be reorganized for continued activity, basing this recommendation on the belief that the company's future lay in distilling. He therefore counselled the immediate sale of a food subsidiary, the Liberty Yeast Co. A few years later he saw an opportunity to profit by the government's decision to consolidate liquor stocks in fewer places. Alcohol still had to be distilled for medical purposes, and in 1927 the American Medicinal Spirits Co. was formed; it arranged a merger of various liquor interests, thus acquiring substantial quantities of whisky and a number of well-known brand names. The original interest acquired by National Distillers in this consolidation amounted to 35 per cent, but shortly, and largely as a result of the sale of its industrial alcohol business to U.S. Industrial Alcohol, National Distillers was able to take over the entire stock of A.M.S., so that when repeal finally came, National Distillers owned a large stock of whisky, several distillery plants and in addition a number of valuable brand names such as Old Grand Dad, Old Taylor, Old Crow, Old Overholt and Mount Vernon. No firm could have been better equipped to meet the great demand for rye and Bourbon that followed repeal. There was no firm with which Gilbey's could have more fortunately allied itself when it decided to enter the American market, not as an importer but with a home-made product.

Today National Distillers market Gilbey's London Gin in the United States, which is one of the most popular brands in the country. The large distillery in Cincinnati puts out well over a million cases in a year.

A later chapter will record the launching in England of Smirnoff vodka, but it may be appropriate to mention here, in discussing the United States, that National Distillers also market the firm's vodka there, under the name of Gilbey's—thus attaching to vodka the goodwill earned by the gin—and in competition, by one of the curiosities of world commerce, with the Smirnoff for which Gilbey's has the British, but not the American, market. Vodka enjoys an enormous vogue in the United States, satisfying the national liking for a clean, strong and odourless 'hard liquor' with which to give a kick to the sweet, soft drinks that are so popular. One has mentioned a curiosity of commerce: it is, surely, a curiosity of the cold war that a Russian drink—indeed, *the* Russian drink—should have become so much a favourite, and so quickly, in the stronghold of the Western way of life.

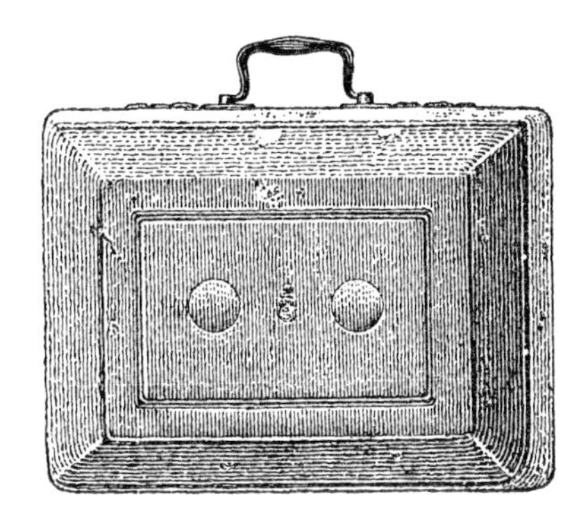

CHAPTER XIII

Trade Relations

MANY of the problems that Gilbey's have had to face during the last fifty years have been those of the wine and spirit trade as a whole. And although light table wines have now and again been granted a concession, almost all Chancellors of the Exchequer have regarded the trade in general as being like the Road Fund—a treasure chest to be raided—and it has been for the most part in vain that its members have argued that if you tax a commodity beyond a certain point, consumption will decrease.

The increase in duties on wine during recent years has been steady and substantial. In 1860 Gladstone fixed the import duty on French table wines at 1*s.* a gallon. It remained at this level until 1899, when it was raised to 1*s.* 3*d.* At the same time the duty on 'dessert' or fortified wines—port and sherry—was raised to 3*s.* per gallon, the dividing line being 30° of proof spirit. Until quite recent years these wines of under 30° were referred to by senior members of the trade as 'Shilling Duty' wines.

In 1920 there was a further increase to 2*s.* 6*d.* and 6*s.* respectively, with a preferential duty of 1*s.* 6*d.* and 4*s.* for Empire wines, a level that was not disturbed until 1927, when the dividing line of strength was reduced to 25° proof spirit on foreign wines and 27° on Empire wines, the duties being 4*s.* per gallon on foreign table wines and 2*s.* on Empire; on dessert wines they were 8*s.* and 4*s.* respectively.

The outbreak of World War II brought further increases, and from 1940 onwards they were steadily increased, until in 1948 they stood at 25*s.* and 50*s.* respectively on foreign wines, and 23*s.* and 40*s.* on Empire. In 1949, however, the new Chancellor of the Exchequer, Sir Stafford Cripps, emulated Mr. Gladstone and reduced the duty on foreign table wines to 13*s.* per gallon, with a similar reduction of 12*s.* on Empire wines.

The duty on dessert wines remained, however, at the very high figure of 50*s.* for foreign and 40*s.* for Empire wines, a rate of duty that at the time of writing is having an unfortunate effect upon the port and even on the sherry trade.

The duties that have been levelled upon spirits have been far more drastic even than those on wines. Mr. Gladstone in 1860 fixed the basic rate at 10*s.* per proof gallon. There were increases of 6*d.* per gallon in 1890 and 1900, until what was then regarded as a staggering increase of 3*s.* 9*d.* per proof gallon was made in 1909. The consternation produced by this increase was so great that Gilbey's directors seriously considered the question of closing down the business, believing that the public could never afford to bear this increased burden. They eventually overcame their qualms and the results did not prove as disastrous as they feared; the duty remained at 14*s.* 9*d.* until 1918, when it was increased to 30*s.*; in 1919 it became 50*s.* and in 1920, 72*s.* 6*d.*

Once the post-war boom had subsided, this high rate caused a decline in the consumption of spirits. The trade began to feel that the burden was intolerable and could not be long supported, but the war in 1939 imposed further burdens and from 1940 onwards, as in the case of wines, steep increases were imposed, the duty rising to 97*s.* 6*d.* in 1940, 137*s.* 6*d.* in 1942, 157*s.* 6*d.*

in 1943, 190*s.* 10*d.* in 1947; in 1948 it reached the extraordinary and, to most people, undreamed-of figure of 210*s.* per gallon.

The difficulties to which the trade has been thus exposed have led inevitably to much co-operation between individual firms and interests, and Gilbey's have always been closely linked with trade association activities. Henry Parry Gilbey was one of the founders of the Wine and Spirit Trade Benevolent Society. Sir Charles Gold was the first president of the Off-Licence Association; Alfred Gilbey and Alec Gold have been chairmen of the Wine and Spirit Association, and Alec Gold has been its president.

Between the wars, Gilbey's association with the trade protection movement became even closer. Ronald Gilbey, who in 1929 had succeeded Arthur Gilbey as president of the Off-Licence Federation, began taking the presidencies of individual retail organizations, both those with off-licences and those with on-licences. During the period between 1927—when he took his first retail presidency of the South-East London Licenced Victuallers' Association—until the outbreak of war he had taken the presidential chairs of more than a hundred associations throughout the country. Not only was he president of the majority of the societies comprising the London Central Board, of which organization he himself took the chair at their annual banquet in June 1929, but he officiated at Nottingham, Birmingham, Cardiff, Plymouth, Leeds, Liverpool, Bristol, Portsmouth and Brighton. He owed his popularity at these functions not to his position as chairman of a leading firm but to the fact that he was one of the most amusing and unusual speakers. It was said of him that he was one of the very few people who should be allowed to tell a funny story in an after-dinner speech. He also identified himself very closely with the trade benevolent movement and was Chairman of the Licensed Victuallers' Benevolent Institution in 1930. In these activities he was followed by his son, Ronnie, the present chairman, who has held some sixty presidential chairs in trade protection associations, which have appreciated his exceptional gifts. He has been ably supported in this important work by James Trimmer, sales manager since 1945.

These trade protection activities were a natural result of the unique position which the liquor trade holds in regard to legislation; and in one respect their necessity is to be deplored—it is a pity that there was so acute a need for them but they have had at least one happy sequel: they have given directors of the company a chance of making the acquaintance of many of its customers.

Their work was made the pleasanter by the fact that a former secretary of the company, C. R. Venner, was honorary secretary of the National Federation of Off-Licence Holders' Associations of England and Wales.

CHAPTER XIV

Advertising

NO new line today can hope to succeed unless its launching is backed with a vigorous publicity campaign. But in the eighteen-sixties transatlantic methods were unknown in England, and the Gilbeys relied upon catalogues and price lists and small notices in the press. There was no appeal to the eye; no elaborate lay-out; no window displays. There was no need for them in those early years. Each individual agent was a separate salesman, dealing in his own way with his special clientèle. The Gilbeys did not consider that it was any part of their business to appeal to the public over the head of the agent. They were not then, as they are now, the owners of proprietary brands of gin, port and sherry, Spey Royal and Red Breast whisky and Odds-On cocktail—brands that have become and that have to be maintained as household words by constant, and constantly varied, reminders to the public, in the face of competition which is also constantly appealing to the consumer with fresh and lively copy and visual images. It was not until 1912, when they put 'Invalid Port' upon the market, that they broke into that field. The 'Invalid Port' campaign was so successful, in a mere half-generation interrupted by four years of war, that in 1926 a Yorkshire newspaper headed with:

Port for Invalids
Stipendiary's Keen Wit

the story of a Hull shopkeeper called Gilbey who, summoned for debt, defended himself by saying that he couldn't pay his own way when he had to allow so much tick in his little general store. 'I have heard of Gilbey's Invalid Port,' said the stipendiary (with a greater display of judicial awareness, if not much more wit, than the judge who asked 'Who is Connie Gilchrist?')—'but *you* seem to be a port for invalids.' But from the launching of the 'Invalid Port' campaign onwards Gilbey's advertisements have been varied and original. Distinguished artists and copy-writers have served the firm, and it is fascinating to turn over Gilbey's old albums and be reminded of the various cartoons and captions that caught the eye and held the attention during the 'twenties and 'thirties. Since 1928 Gilbey's advertising has been in the hands of Alfred Pemberton Limited.

It was a period of transition in the advertiser's art. Along with the bulbous lettering and the thickly outlined figures that had been the commonplaces of poster art and other displays since the turn of the century (John Hassall's 'Skegness is so Bracing' is the classic example), and that continued until the outbreak of World War II—perhaps the two best, among Gilbey's posters, are Cooper's galloping racehorse, based on a nineteenth-century print, and his line of peasants in the Douro vineyards—one comes across something as fresh and as contemporary in feeling as McKnight Kauffer's effectively simple poster for 'Invalid Port', designed in 1933, and still vivid and arresting in its use of formal design, sprayed colour and space. Many of the designs executed for Gilbey's by this genius of applied art were lent by the Company to the Victoria and Albert Museum for its memorial exhibition of McKnight Kauffer's work in 1955.

Retailers demanded something more conventional, though, than McKnight Kauffer in the way of window-cards, and it is odd to notice how in this branch of applied art, if in no other, the tendency over the past quarter of a century has been towards greater realism. The flatly painted, flat-chested girl of the nineteen-twenties has yielded place to a more buxom maiden, portrayed in colour-photography instead of poster paint, holding out very often a three-dimensional glass for another helping of Gilbey's port.

Outside the windows of the off-licence shops, where tradition rules firmly and long, the firm has been able to be more enterprising in breaking new ground. Just as McKnight Kauffer was commissioned to design posters in the nineteen-thirties so, in the nineteen-fifties, Milner Gray, one of the most distinguished of contemporary designers, was appointed Consulting Designer to the company to carry through a complete redesign programme of all their materials, bottles, labels, capsules, stoppers, stationery, cartons, lists, lorries—in fact, to establish, in the public eye, a positive and controlled House style. His bottle labels are based on rococo eighteenth-century motifs for table wines; on colour prints of the early nineteenth century for rum; and on a new rounded-corner shape, and a mixture of the square lettering and flowing script of the early nineteenth century (with the elegant clarity of many a church's memorial tablets) for ports and sherries.

In an article by Norbert Dutton in *Design* (the journal of the Council of Industrial Design) for July 1955 two of Milner Gray's labels for Gilbey's bottles were the full-page initial illustration, and the article ended with the paragraph:

> Milner Gray's distinguished work for W. & A. Gilbey Ltd. is therefore welcome, not only for its intrinsic interest, but as a demonstration of the 'timeless' quality of good design. Richly decorative yet executed with a formal restraint, these wine labels reflect the experience and skill that go into the making of the product, and dispose effectively of the idea that good packaging is a mere adjunct to the promotion of cheap and competitive merchandise.

At the same time, W. M. de Majo was appointed as Design Consultant in the field of Exhibitions and Display and this combination of contrasting talents has, in three years, raised the Company to a leading position among those in industry who devote care and taste to product presentation at all levels.

Packaging and labelling have been designed and developed, in fact, in the belief, expressed in an internal memorandum, 'that the label on every product is a small-scale poster site, advertising the merits and quality of the brand, and that good design results in good business'. The effectiveness of this policy can be seen, in a small compass, at Hunter's in Berkeley Street, where the stock consists largely of Gilbey's wines and spirits, and where modern shop-fitting design and lighting effectively show off modern design in packaging without losing anything of the traditional dignity of a West End wine merchant's establishment.

These principles, applied to the newest lines as well as the oldest—to a new Irish whiskey, for instance; and to a new tonic wine, which inherited the word 'Invalid' from the 'Invalid Port' of between the wars *—and to all materials used and sponsored by the company, from delivery lorry to bottle capsule, won recognition for the company and their designers in the United States and in France: the only British company to get an award (an honourable mention) in the U.S. Package Designers' Council 1954 list; with an invitation to show some of the work in an exhibition of the Alliance Graphique Internationale at the Louvre.

Also displayed at the Louvre was material from *The Compleat Imbiber*, a light-hearted magazine launched in 1953 and devoted to the amusement and instruction of customers and friends at home and abroad—to the tune of 12,000 copies of each of the two-a-year issues, half of which went overseas. Some of the most distinguished yet lively writers and artists continue to contribute

* Shortly after the war, the Ministry of Food, in a praiseworthy but not always well-advised attempt to abolish misleading trade descriptions of foods and drinks, which sometimes led to interference with long-established and well-understood trade marks and general descriptions (the Ministry was laughed out of its proposed interference with the sherry 'Bristol Cream', but succeeded in modifying the term 'digestive' for biscuits), laid it down successfully that a port, as such, could not be branded 'Invalid', though Gilbey's Invalid Port had been known for more than a generation. However, 'Invalid Port' became Gilbey's Triple Crown, and the firm decided to apply the word 'Invalid' to a tonic wine containing specified quantities of vitamins.

to these gay pages, an anthology from which was presented by Putnams to a wider public at Christmas 1956, and which won prizes offered for magazines of its kind in Britain and the United States.

More serious and perhaps more ambitious was the documentary film *The Song of the Grape*, commissioned by the firm in 1953: filmed during 1954 in Portugal, selected for showing at the Edinburgh Film Festival in 1955 and distributed commercially in 1956—a rare honour for a documentary film—by the Rank Organization.

Conceived and produced by Antony Grinling, a director of Gilbey's, the film was directed by John Stewart, and music was specially composed for it by Elizabeth Lutyens. Norman Shelley spoke the commentary written by C. Gordon Glover. The film, filled with sunshine and with the life of a peasant people, begins by showing the breaking-up of the rocky soil of the Douro valley, so that the vines can be planted. Men and women march through the villages to take part in the vintage in the Quinta da Roeda, 'the Diamond in the Ring', whence come the grapes for Gilbey's port. The rhythm of the seasons, and of the life of the vine, dominate the film.

It was a tribute to the effectiveness of Gilbey's advertising, and an appropriate recognition of the firm's interest in modern design and commercial art, that it should have been awarded the concession for the restaurants and bars at the Festival of Britain on the South Bank in 1951 and for the Festival Gardens at Battersea. Born just too late for the Great Exhibition at the Crystal Palace in 1851, the firm was demonstrably at the top of its trade at the Great Exhibition of a century later.

CHAPTER XV

The Move to Oval Road

COLONEL Alfred Gilbey had said in his speech at the war-memorial ceremony at the Pantheon in 1920:

> This building which we are now in I suppose may be considered to stand in one of the greatest shopping centres of the world. We have often been approached to sell the building. It has been pointed out to us that it might be more advantageous to the working of the business if our offices and stores were under one roof. It has also been said that in business there should be no sentiment. We do not agree with that theory. This place is full of associations—it holds the memories of our fathers and those who sat round those desks in bygone days, who helped to build up this business, and these tablets [he pointed to the war memorial] will further strengthen the bond that binds us to this old and historic building.

The speech was applauded loudly, but within a dozen years or so it had become very clear that the pressure of necessity was too great even for a sentiment so sincerely felt and eloquently expressed.

The period between the two great wars, in spite of slumps and unemployment, was one of progress, prosperity and rapidly expanding business for Gilbey's, and midway through the nineteen-thirties the necessity became apparent of having the administrative offices conveniently close to the bonded warehouse and bottling departments. In James Street, Camden Town, on the edge of Regent's Park, the site of an old public house had become available, and it was decided to build here a modern eight-storey block of administrative offices that could serve all the warehouses in the large group of buildings, all near by, which the firm controlled. Serge Chermayeff was chosen as the architect—then only in his early thirties but already one of the most distinguished artists in the modern idiom of Gropius, le Corbusier and Mendelsohn. On this new work, in fact, he enjoyed the veteran Mendelsohn's advice and assistance. The same two architects worked together on another distinguished piece of modern architecture, the De la Warr Pavilion at Bexhill.

On March 19, 1937, the head office moved from the Pantheon into a building that apart from its artistic qualities, which are high, is of considerable constructional, as distinct from aesthetic, interest from the functional completeness of its equipment and the success with which it has been soundproofed.

Each floor was planned as the unit of a particular department. Thus, the basement houses the records and the strong room, the ground floor contains the staff and managers' canteens. The first floor is the Purchasing Department, with a striking sample room. The second floor, Sales and Advertising Departments. The third floor, Export Department. The fourth and fifth, Finance Department, Ledger, Traffic and Invoicing Departments and the Company's Secretary. The top floor is the directors' floor, where Board Room and Committee Room are placed high up away from noise, with a superb view over London. Here also the directors can lunch, a return to the old days at the Pantheon, when big lunch parties of the directors and their friends were held, and parties from Camden Town led by Henry Grinling arrived in four-wheeler cabs. In those

Victorian days, the menu was generally the same on 'big occasions'—fried sole, Surrey capons, rice pudding and, when in season, strawberries. Nowadays, the directors eat more lightly but range more widely.

The new building, its reinforced concrete painted in the lightest of shades, is described by Nikolaus Pevsner (the 1956 Reith lecturer on 'The Englishness of English Art') in his *London*, published in 1952, as being 'remarkably good modern, 1937, a corner site, with one front slightly broken so as to appear curved, the other provided with an angular bay window projecting over the main entrance. The building is of reinforced concrete, with a ground floor faced with brown glazed tiles, and all windows teak-framed.' Mr. Pevsner is an authority of the greatest eminence, and his description is accurate enough, but it fails to convey the delighted surprise with which one comes upon the clean lines and functional elegance, the suggestion both of lightness and of light, of the new building in a grimy Camden Town corner of the railway age.

Inside, the woodwork used for the panelling of the Board Room and for the directors' furniture is of Australian walnut. The general office furniture and equipment is of steel. The most modern devices for comfort and convenience have been installed, and it is air-conditioned, and insulated from noise and vibration, by being mounted on a compressed cork foundation. The staircase, lift enclosure and cloakrooms have been placed in the 'dead' space at the north-east corner of the site and are ventilated by wells between the new and the old buildings. A portion of one of the adjacent original warehouses has been adapted to accommodate two model shop windows in which window display schemes are worked out.

At the actual moment of the move there were inevitably those who regretted leaving the historic Pantheon; but for all its picturesqueness the building was no longer adequate for the demands of a modern and expanding business: and apart from the additional amenities that the staff now enjoys, the change has made possible a complete reorganization of factory and bottling procedure. Moreover, the old building had never been comfortable in winter. At first a large stove stood in its centre, built in 1850, but it never worked efficiently. Its two fireplaces were 'encouraged' by a down-draught created by fires lit in the basement and an east wind filled the hall with smoke. When central heating was installed with pipes along the ceiling, the glass roof created down-draughts of cold air.

It was lucky that the firm should have decided to build when it did. Thirty months later it would have been too late. Between September 1939 and December 1954 no substantial building operations, except those for which a certain degree of national importance could be claimed, were allowed to be undertaken; valuable though Gilbey's contribution was to the nation's cheer and comfort, it is unlikely that the Ministry of Works could have been persuaded to consider the firm's activities in that light. As things turned out, the house was well equipped to cope with the six years of trial.

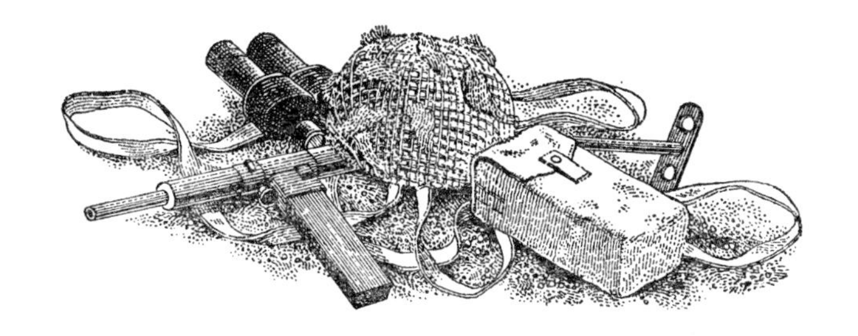

CHAPTER XVI

World War II

NO doubt the second generation of Gilbeys and Blyths and Golds and Grinlings had considered that the First World War imposed heavy demands upon their reserves, resources and organization. But those demands were slight in comparison with the strain that was inflicted upon the third generation during World War II. After the Munich Pact of 1938, when it became clear that a second world war was probable, Gilbey's did their best to protect themselves by an increase of imports, so that September 1939 found them with abnormally large stocks of wine. But no measure of foresight could have procured immunity against the series of catastrophes that befell Europe in the summer of 1940. After the collapse of France, no wine could be obtained from the Bordeaux merchants; ships could no longer put in at Spain and Portugal; many cellars and warehouses were destroyed by bombing; submarine attacks made the importation of grain extremely difficult; and barley, the raw material of Scotch whisky, had to be diverted from the distilleries to the feeding of livestock. Finally, in 1942, the distillation of Scotch whisky ceased altogether.

Gilbey's were, perhaps, more fortunate than many of their colleagues. Only two bombs fell on the bottle warehouse next to Gilbey House and the old and firmly-built structure withstood the shock. The depots at Plymouth, Bristol and Cardiff were demolished, and some 30,000 gallons of rum that had been moved to Bow for safety were destroyed. At Southampton, at Above Bar, the depot was the only building left standing.

The behaviour of the wine trade during these years did credit to a community whose reputation in this country for square dealing has always stood enviably high. No attempt was made to make unfair profits out of an exceptional situation. Each firm considered the extent of its stocks in the light of the needs of its customers; the amount it had paid for the wine; the interest that had accrued; the increased cost of living; and then estimated a fair price. The quota system was evolved. Each month the customer received a parcel. A new regard grew up for a commodity rather than for its name, and the wine merchant, instead of saying that he had bought a certain consignment, would genially remark, 'I think I shall be able to let you have a dozen half-bottles of red wine this month.'

It should not be left unrecorded that in these difficult times the Ministry of Food, then under Lord Woolton, gave the fullest co-operation to the representatives of the Wine and Spirit Association, once again under the chairmanship of that well-loved friend of wine, Colonel Ian Campbell. As a result of that co-operation, the 'concession' system was evolved, by which as shipping became available—a troopship, for example, returning empty from the Middle East—imports from various countries were allowed. Some curious beverages found their way by this system to British tables: a bottle was a bottle. But the wine trade was kept going and conviviality was not allowed to perish from the earth. At first these concessions were small, but as the tide of battle turned, first Algerian and then French wines became available, and in the summer of 1944 Gilbey's were at last able to make enquiries as to what had happened to their property in France.

The Atlantic seaboard had been occupied by the Germans after July 1940, and Château Loudenne, as enemy property, had been sequestrated. But Camille Gombeau, now far too old for military service, had been left in charge, and was permitted by the Germans to remain and watch over the House's interests with skill and loyalty.

At the beginning of the war, there was at the Château a big stock of spirits, which he sold to provide himself with working capital. There were few 'incidents' in Bordeaux and he saw, in fact, extremely little of the Germans. Occasionally a group of staff officers would motor out to picnic on the terrace, and once a colonel with romantic aptitudes made use of the Château for his weekend rendezvous. But, for the most part, Gombeau was left undisturbed to carry on as best he could. The shortage of labour, materials, and particularly chemical manures and insecticides, made his task difficult, but he managed to produce 111 hogsheads in 1941; 48 in 1942; 41 in 1943; and 82 in 1944.

In 1943–44 the Germans, after losing the rich wheatfields of the Ukraine to the counter-attacking Russians, decided to plant a section of the estate with corn. A squad of twenty prisoners of war from North Africa were instructed to dig up the vines, and a French collaborator was installed as manager, over Gombeau. The prisoners were eventually rescued by the maquis and the collaborator was lucky to escape alive across the frontier.

During all this time, Camille Gombeau had received only one piece of news about the London office and that a disturbing one, a cable from his brother-in-law in Lisbon reporting 'All Gilbey directors dead'. The message should have read 'Old Gilbey directors dead'. Gombeau for several months was under the impression that a bomb had landed in the Board room at Oval Road. He had never expected to be able to welcome his old friend Gordon Gilbey back to Château Loudenne.

On the whole, the situation in Bordeaux was not as serious as the directors had often feared that it would prove to be. Eventually, they even picked up the tracks of a large and valuable stock of cognac brandies that had been stored under the custody of Messrs. T. Hine & Co., of Jarnac. The fate of this stock provides a typical example of German thoroughness and respect for order. The property of an English firm was, of course, subject to sequestration, but although the entire stock was requisitioned, meticulous records were left of the amounts taken, and the names of the German merchants to whom the brandy was sent, and later a French government office in Paris wrote, 'out of the blue', to state that they had taken over a German organization which had opened an account in the name of W. & A. Gilbey Ltd., showing that several millions of francs were awaiting instructions for disposal. The old brandies were irreplaceable; the francs had lost their value; but the firm might have fared far worse.

At the same time, Château Loudenne was a very definite problem in 1946; not only had many of the vines been pulled up by the Germans to make way for corn, but for six and a half years there had been no new planting, and many of the vines were in bad condition. The Médoc had been one of the last German pockets of resistance and the Château had been heavily shaken by bombs. Repairs were urgently required. Not only was the cost of such repairs likely to be extremely high, but it was doubtful whether the Bank of England would allow the firm to transfer sufficient funds to carry out this highly necessary work.

In spite of these difficulties, however, the restoring of the property has been undertaken; in 1950, 314 hogsheads were produced, and in the autumn of 1952 was held the first post-war party for the *vendange.*

The occasion was the launching of white Gravette, which was then being put upon the market at six-and-six a bottle, and some twenty members of the Press made the excursion, with Ian Mackay as the doyen of the party.

It was a great success. The guests found much to interest, much to surprise them too. There was far less bustle than they had expected. There was an air of emptiness about the property, not only because fewer acres were under cultivation, but because owing to mechanical improvements there were fewer workmen in the vineyards. Shortage of labour has been a problem for thirty years. The young not only prefer to live in towns but demand better living conditions than those which their grandparents accepted gratefully. They expect a four- instead of a two-roomed cottage, and new time- and labour-saving devices have been installed in all the modern vineyards.

Much that was traditional was shown to the Press party—the women snipping the bunches, the tipping of the baskets into the large shoulder buckets which the *porteurs* empty into huge tubs drawn to the *chais* by dun-coloured, slow-moving oxen—the

Bottle Warehouse adjacent to Regent's Canal

Gilbey's Four-in-Hand. Exercise turnout

'sacrificial victims' of which the old Roman poet wrote. A Roman need not have felt that he had returned to an alien world could he have strolled beside Raymond Postgate through the narrow alleys of the vine-rows. At the same time, Alfred Gilbey could never have foreseen that the work of the estate would one day be carried on by a mere dozen families.

The traditional procedure of wine-making is still carried on, except that the *Agrappoir* now replaces treading to separate the grapes from the stalks and give a slight crush to the grapes before entering the fermenting vat.

At Château Loudenne, where large quantities of white wines are produced in addition to the red—white is somewhat exceptional in the Médoc—modern, barrel-shaped, electrically-operated presses have been installed, replacing the old hand-operated ratchet presses, capable of dealing with three hundred gallons of white wine an hour and with the pressing of the marc (pulp) of red wine so efficiently that not a drop of liquid produced by the grape goes to waste. In other directions, too, there has been a cutting down of labour. For many years no wine has been bottled at the Château, except a few litres of red wine that the partners keep for their own use; all wine has been shipped in cask to be bottled in London, because of the great advantage in duty that is enjoyed by wine imported in cask as against wine in bottle; now, however, some is being transported in tankers, a further economy of time and labour, and the tram-lines running down from the *chais* to the little port on the Gironde are overgrown with grass.

Alfred Gilbey and James Blyth would have found much to make them wonder, could they have watched Gordon Gilbey showing the Press party round the estate. So many things are different, but they would have found no difference in the spirit of welcome with which the guests were welcomed at the Château. A *cordon-bleu* chef and a staff of servants were requisitioned from Bordeaux, and Margaux 1875 was selected as the most prized possession in the private cellar. Camille Gombeau decanted the wine himself, and twelve bottles were opened before he found six that satisfied his exacting standard. The Margaux '75 followed a Gravette and a château-bottled Loudenne of '24. Raymond Postgate referred in his after-dinner speech to Loudenne's 'geranium flavour': and everyone was impressed both with its smoothness and its body. Loudenne wine is not officially classified among the five principal 'growths' of the Médoc, but it should be remembered that the last standard classification of the growths of the Médoc was made in 1855, and that in a hundred years the wines of some châteaux have improved, while those of others have deteriorated. The company that evening left the table convinced that if there were a reclassification today, Loudenne, were it to be represented before the judges by its château-bottled '24s and '29s, could hardly fail to earn a place of honour.

After the banquet, the guests were taken down into the village to attend the *bal du vendange.* There was no lack there of bustle. The town hall was crowded: there was an excellent performance of local dances, and a bar was kept supplied with flagons of Gravette. The last revellers were not home till three o'clock. Though practically every phase of culture except the gathering and pruning has now been mechanized, the traditional gay spirit of *la vendange* has been maintained.

Ian Mackay was the doyen of the party. The son of a crofter; tall, leonine, with a thick crop of greying hair, he had an ageless quality. His enjoyment of his time at Château Loudenne was manifest. In an article for the *News Chronicle,* among the last he was to write, Mackay spoke of the Château's 'fine, sleek claret and a Gravette of dancing piquancy'.

CHAPTER XVII

1945

IN Britain, more than in any other belligerent country, the conditions of wartime discomfort long survived the end of the war.

For the wine trade in particular there was little change for several months. Wine was still a 'concession' commodity. Not till the end of 1949 was importation under an open general licence permitted. At the end of 1945 limited licences were issued for the purchase of barley for the distillation of Scotch whisky, but only on a quota basis. Full distillation was not resumed until the end of 1948, and even then, as far as the individual customer was concerned, the situation remained unchanged. The quota system was retained, Scotch whisky being one of the biggest dollar-earning commodities exported from Great Britain, with discussions taking place each year between the Scotch Whisky Association and the Ministry of Food to decide what quantity must be used for export and how much could be released for the home market. For the average Briton, VJ Day 1945 did not bring the curtain down on the conditions that war had created.

It did, however, except on certain limited fronts, mean an end of fighting: it meant partial demobilization, and as regards the House of Gilbey it meant the entry of the fourth generation.

In the nineteen-thirties three young Gilbeys had joined the firm: Derek, the grandson of the second Sir Walter; Ronald, the son of Ronald and great-grandson of Alfred Gilbey; and another great-grandson of Alfred, John, son of Gordon and grandson of William Crosbie Gilbey. These three all joined the Services, while two other members of the fourth generation, Arthur, the son of Sebastian Gilbey, and Jasper, the son of Antony Grinling, though they were still too young to have joined the firm, also served through the war in uniform.

Curiously enough, three members of this group had an unfortunate similarity of experience in being taken prisoner. Derek Gilbey was captured in Crete, with the Black Watch in January 1941, and remained in Germany until after the war, succeeding to his grandfather's baronetcy while a prisoner of war. Arthur Gilbey, who served in the Middle East with the 4th Queen's Own Hussars, was captured in Greece in August 1941. He escaped at the time of the Italian Armistice but was recaptured three months later and was held in Germany until April 1945. Jasper Grinling, who served with the 12th Royal Lancers in the Italian campaign of 1943–44, was captured on patrol north of Bologna in the autumn of 1944.

John Gilbey had a luckier but very strenuous war. Starting as as private in the H.A.C., he served two years in Iceland as a subaltern in the Duke of Wellington's Regiment, being later attached to a Photo Recce Unit for six months in Egypt and eighteen months in Italy; he was demobilized with the rank of major.

Ronald Gilbey, who was an equipment officer in the R.A.F.V.R., was invalided out of the service in September 1941.

All five of this group were at their desks in Oval Road by the middle of 1946, so that the pattern of young men returning from the wars to business which had been set by Walter and Alfred Gilbey in 1856 and had been resumed by the third generation in 1919 was now carried on by the fourth. A sixth member of the fourth generation, Alec Gold's son, Robin, who had been too young for military service, joined the firm a little later: there were therefore at Oval Road at the turn of the half-century seven grandsons and six great-grandsons of the original partners.

The growth of the business may be seen in the rise in the figure for gross tangible assets. Standing at £2,000,000 at the outbreak of World War I these had reached £2,750,000 by 1923, in spite of the writing off of goodwill from reserves to the tune of nearly £750,000. In the last year before World War II the assets stood at £4,250,000 and now the company enters 1957 at a figure of £10,000,000.

CHAPTER XVIII

The Fourth Generation

TO the fourth generation, as to the third, contemporary conditions have presented a whole new set of problems. Shortage of money had by 1950 removed the need of rationing, except for whisky, so that a man could drink as much as he could afford. Lack of money, however, as the result of high taxation, and the high duties imposed on wine and spirits had forced economical habits upon the public. But the foundations of Gilbey's prosperity today are not only as stable now as they were in 1939, but on every side there are signs of expansion, development and the consolidation of newly-won territories.

The story of how that has been accomplished can be seen in the course of a half-hour's examination of the sample room. Its shelves carry exhibit bottles of each of the House's products and these bottles explain the strategy of the last decade. There are two main branches of activity, the increase and development of overseas markets, and the discovery for the home market of new sound lines, both in terms of wine and spirits.

The export trade is, in a sense, the more interesting because it is new. Gilbey's activities are now world-wide: they have established plants in Canada, Australia, South Africa and the United States, and the shelves contain many items that are not available in the United Kingdom. There are, for example, three different kinds of rye whisky: Golden Velvet, Black Velvet and Golden Special, that are only sold in Canada. For the Australian market also there are three different kinds of Australian whisky: Castle Malt, Gauntlet and Bond 7—the last a very fine liqueur. Scotch whisky is becoming popular in sophisticated homes and bars in France too, perhaps through American influence. There is also an Irish whiskey, Crock o' Gold, which has been specially blended for the American palate, and which was introduced to Dublin at the same time as the reopening of the company's remodelled premises in O'Connell Street, with their beautiful mahogany doors and plaster mouldings—a house that has belonged to the firm since 1864, and in which Lord Blyth had presided over much typically ample Victorian entertaining.

The preparation of this Irish whiskey is one of Gilbey's most ambitious enterprises. For many years its Dublin Branch had been aware that the straight pot-still whiskeys traditionally enjoyed in Ireland were less popular in other countries, particularly in North America. After various experiments in blending, it arranged with the appropriate government authorities to make available for transit passengers at the duty-free Shannon Airport a lighter blend of spirit. As it had to compete with the well-known and expensively-dressed whiskies and brandies from France and America, a special bottle was designed to proclaim that it contained a traditional Irish product, wrapped in Irish tweed and sealed with a green ribbon. It proved so successful in this narrow field that it was decided to launch a campaign to popularize it in America. The trend of taste on the other side of the Atlantic has been for some time now for lighter kinds of whisky, and 'light' is the adjective that has been stressed in the publicity campaigns launching Crock o' Gold.

In addition to these new brands of whisky, Spey Royal Scotch whisky continues to be one of Gilbey's chief exports, and early in 1954 an arrangement was made with the firm of Bacardi Imports Inc., of New York, for its distribution throughout the

United States. Bacardi's have a strong distribution throughout the United States for their well-known brand of Bacardi rum, and they will now have the future distribution of Spey Royal Scotch whisky in conjunction with their rum, which will prove to be a strong and sound arrangement, by reason of the fact that there will be only two items to be offered throughout the country, the whisky and the rum, whereas many distributors in the United States have such a multiplicity of various brands to offer that concentrated attention and effort cannot be devoted to any single item.

The story of Gilbey's export trade would not be complete without a reference to the close association with the world-famous Vermouth Company—Francesco Cinzano & Cia., of Turin, whose plant in Buenos Aires has distilled Gilbey's Gin for the Argentine market since 1930. The original agreement has been considerably extended and Cinzano now distil Gilbey's Gin for the markets in Italy, France, Spain, Argentine, Chile and Brazil, while acting as general Agents in Belgium, Germany, Columbia and Cuba.

Gilbey's, in their turn, act as Agents for Cinzano in Canada and Ireland.

This longstanding association owes much to the friendship between the Count Enrico Marone Cinzano—President of Cinzano—and his family and the Gilbey directors. The President has also close ties with Spain; his wife is the Infanta Maria Cristina de Borbon, a daughter of the late King Alfonso of Spain.

This intense drive to enlarge overseas markets has not led to any neglect of the home market, where the demand for whisky, for instance, led to the acquisition of the first bulk-whisky tanker, capable of carrying two thousand gallons, and named by Sir Compton Mackenzie, in a televised ceremony, after his novel and film, *Whisky Galore*, before he wished good luck to what he called 'this magnificent monster, which will travel the roads with this noble liquor'.

Gilbey's gin is as much in demand as ever; the 'Odds-On' wine cocktail is still popular with those who prefer a mild aperitif. Gilbey's are now distributors of Cinzano in three styles, Italian Red, Italian White and French, which ensures that a sound ingredient is blended with their gin, while variety has been sought and found by the launching of Smirnoff vodka.

Vodka had been introduced into Western Europe early in the nineteenth century by Pierre Smirnoff. After the 1917 revolution the Smirnoff family established themselves first in Poland and then in Paris. Vodka had long been regarded in England as a powerful aperitif to be gulped with highly flavoured hors d'œuvre or caviare. Its many possibilities had never been appreciated here till Gilbey's decided to manufacture it in London.

It was launched in the Coronation summer of 1953, to balalaika music, with a party at Oval Road attended by nearly a thousand guests.

Vodka can be drunk straight, out of a small glass, as the Russians drink it, but Westerners have discovered that it is even better as an ingredient in long and short mixed drinks. It is odourless and it has no strong individual flavour, both of which attributes mean that it can mix with practically anything. It is sold in two strengths, White Label at 65·5° proof and Blue Label 80° proof. You can make a vodka Dry Martini; vodka and ginger beer, the Moscow Mule, is excellent. But the two most popular recipes are in cocktail form: the 'Bloody Mary', which is international—it is discreetly called a Red Snapper in Gilbey's list—in which vodka is mixed with iced tomato juice, a dash of Worcester sauce and a squeeze of lemon; and the 'Roberta May', which was a prize-winner in the 1954 world cocktail competition and which consists of one-third vodka, one-third Aurum, an Italian liqueur, and one-third orange squash with a dash of white of egg. Vodka can also be used to give extra 'kick' to an 'Odds-On' cocktail.

The House has not by any means concentrated upon spirits. Sir Stafford Cripps's reduction of the duties on table wines gave them the same opportunity that Gladstone had of supplying a sound palatable wine at a popular price. At the 1954 Ideal Home Exhibition, their stand bore the streamer 'Wine Merchants to the People through Six Reigns' and they were represented by a light red wine—La Tourelle—and a *vin rosé*, as well as the white Gravette mentioned in an earlier chapter; all aroused great interest.

One of the most remarkable developments in English habits since the war has been the growth in the demand for table wines. It is not only that people who used in the old days to drink wine occasionally with their meals have come to drink it more regularly, but that people now drink wine who never did so, or whose parents never did so, before the war. Partly, it is the reflection of a soberer age—there is less drinking for drinking's sake, and more drinking for health's sake, or for the sake of establishing a meal. And that means wines rather than 'hard' liquor. Partly, it is that many more people travel abroad and learn in wine-growing countries to like wine. Some had already done so in the war. Partly, it is the result of advertising campaigns by the wine-growing countries. And the tendency received a tremendous impetus when Sir Stafford Cripps reduced the duties on table wines in 1949.

The most dignified wine merchants, in the most exalted corners of the West End, realized that while there was no steady and substantial profit—though there would always be good business—in château-bottled clarets, vintage ports and the like, because the class that used to buy such fine wines regularly could now only buy them occasionally, as a treat, there was nevertheless a steadier trade than ever, with that class and with a class new to wine-drinking, in simple but good wines at a modest price.

Public demand brought down the prices of wines in bottle and in carafe in all but the most fashionable restaurants, and almost halved them in the restaurant cars of British Railways. Many a simple London pub now advertises wine by the glass, as do a great number of restaurants.

Gilbey's, with their estates at Loudenne, whence they could ship red, white and *rosé* wines in bulk (the difference in price between wine shipped in cask and wine shipped in bottle is just over two shillings a bottle) were naturally pioneers in bringing cheap sound wines to the new wine-drinkers, and to the old wine-drinkers who now have to economize. Their current list shows a red and a white Bordeaux and a *vin rosé* at six shillings and sixpence a bottle, and there are other French wines at seven shillings, and at seven-and-sixpence from South Africa.

The demand by restaurants for good carafe and 'by-the-glass' wines was met by another of Gilbey's innovations: one-gallon glass jars, in unbreakable cylindrical transit cases, in which are supplied Beaujolais, red and white Bordeaux, and *vin rosé*. It could be said, no doubt, that it was the duty of a firm whose fortunes had been founded on supplying wines at a reasonable price to a new class of wine-drinkers, to respond to a similar situation almost a century later. Gilbey's responded.

In the books of newspaper cuttings there are many references to the sustained interest that the House takes in horseflesh. Since the days when the first Sir Walter Gilbey drove to Ascot with a pair of horses ridden by postillions, and the days when the second Sir Walter, in his old age, inveighed against the slovenly sartorial habits of the young who rode in the Park in jodhpurs and high-necked sweaters, the public has always associated the name of Gilbey with carriages and horses. Until August 1914 all town deliveries were made by horse van, but the seventy-two horses in the Gilbey's stables were requisitioned by the War Office. Between the wars only motor vans were used, but now the House has returned to its old allegiance and today horse-drawn delivery vans bearing the name of Gilbey's are as familiar a sight on London streets as the coach in which Scotts of Piccadilly deliver hats to their customers. Sebastian Gilbey drives his four-in-hand to Ascot and his phaeton to the Richmond Horse Show. His four horses are named Spey Royal, Odds-On, Triple Crown and Governor General. He has been consistently successful during the last four years, winning the first prize more than once at the Royal Windsor, Aldershot and Richmond Royal Horse Shows.

Gilbey's horses played a prominent role at the Coronation. The Crown Equerry, Sir Dermot McMorrough Kavanagh, was in despair over the difficulties of mounting the Prime Minister's procession. A wise friend counselled him to 'try Frank Gilbey'. Captain Frank Gilbey, a fox-hunting man who farms in Somerset, a dandy like the first Sir Walter, who owns a valuable collection of coaching prints, undertook the task. He was unable to persuade his cousin, Ronald Gilbey, 'to climb into fancy breeches at *my* age!' but Gilbey's bays, Johnny and Major, driven by Frank Gilbey, drew the Prime Minister's coach, and

Henry Hawkins, the firm's head coachman and whip, drove Paddy and Brandy Royal, who drew the Canadian Prime Minister's. He has driven in the Lord Mayor's Show for six years running, but his service with Gilbey's is all post-war, though he has worked with horses all his life. Percy Eves, on the other hand, the firm's head 'stable lad', was carriage-groom for Sir Walter Gilbey at Elsenham Hall from 1907 to 1910, when he entered the service of the company: he reached retiring age in 1953 but was asked to stay on as head stable lad because of his vast experience. He can remember when there were twelve stablemen and seventy-three horses, seventy-two of which were called up for service in 1914. In those days, single-horse vans used to draw whisky and wines from the warehouses for daily deliveries to the docks.

The company started again with horses in 1947, with one pair; now there are seven horses, two coachmen, two footmen and Eves himself.

If it is Sebastian Gilbey who, in dress and manner and tastes, has most obviously inherited the family passion for horses—he drives to the offices in Oval Road sometimes in the coach, sometimes in the exercising-wagon, but always handling four horses; and he has hunted with seventeen packs of foxhounds and two of staghounds—there is a strong tradition among his kinsmen and fellow-directors of keenness on games and on sport. Sir Derek Gilbey is a keen racegoer, and the chairman, A. R. D. Gilbey, besides being a London County Councillor, is a noted skater and an international judge of skating. John Gilbey—son of Gordon, who as a connoisseur of wines is eminent even in the wine trade—has played Rugby football for Ampleforth and the Harlequins. Arthur Gilbey, the vice-chairman, Sebastian's son, and a trustee of Glyndebourne, played racquets for Harrow and golf for Oxford; Derek Blyth was in the Harrow XI, and Alec Gold was a cricketer, having played for the Eton Ramblers and the M.C.C. He is also a keen golfer and is married to a lady international. Jasper Grinling was Captain of Harrow racquets and now devotes his spare time to being a Sunday painter; he carries on a family tradition of the Grinlings, for his father Antony, is a sculptor and wood-carver of considerable distinction, having exhibited not only at the

Royal Academy but also among the 'Artists of Fame and Promise' at the Leicester Galleries.

These, then, are the ten present directors (Alec Gold's son, Robin, will soon join the board) and they are the present custodians of the House of Gilbey, confident that whatever changes of taste may supervene, the House of Gilbey will be competent and equipped to cope with them.

Honoured by the Royal Warrants of Queen Victoria, Edward VII, George V and George VI, with its assets estimated at ten millions sterling, with its vineyards on the Gironde, with its large stocks at Jerez and Oporto; its distilleries in Melbourne, Toronto, Pietermaritzburg and Cincinnati; with its agencies in every country, it is able in the shortest possible time to obtain wine from and deliver it to any required point.

The lesson of the early nineteenth-century coach driver has been thoroughly absorbed. It was in terms of that absorption that Henry Gilbey's sons within two years of opening their business had turned the threat of complete failure into the promise of supreme success, and if the ghosts of Walter and Alfred Gilbey could return today to Oval Road, they would not find so very much there to surprise them. The building of the firm's fortunes has continued on the lines that they themselves laid down. They would find much to give them a sense of pride and fulfilment; but what very certainly would please them most, more than the filing cabinets and the warehouses, the calculating machinery and the distilleries, the clatter of packing cases and the hum of engines, would be the atmosphere of the directors' lunch-room.

Every day at one o'clock there is a gathering in the Sample Room for a glass of sherry or a cocktail; most of the directors will be there; one or two of them will have brought a guest. There will be ten minutes or so of chatter, then a move to the dining-room, with its great view over London, very green and leafy from this height—to a long narrow table with curved ends; on a sideboard, under hot covers, is the *plat du jour*, very probably a joint; wine will be served, and the meal will end with cheese and fruit; a decanter of port making its traditional circuit of the table. The talk during lunch is general; and throughout the year more talk is devoted to cricket, golf and racing than to 'shop' or politics. The atmosphere would be very sympathetic, particularly to Walter Gilbey, who would be pleased to see at one end of the modern room a portrait of his elder brother and benefactor, Henry Parry Gilbey, and at the other a picture by Norman Wilkinson, more modern than the portrait but in the old tradition, of a fly-fisherman on the Spey, and one by Lionel Edwards (traditional indeed!) of the Gilbey coach in Regent's Park in 1953 with the late Ronald Gilbey driving and Sebastian aboard.

But what would please the first Sir Walter and his brothers most would be the sight round the table of the grandsons and the great-grandsons of the men with whom they had started their venture a century ago; Gilbey, and Blyth, and Gold, and Grinling—the same four names, not one dropped out and not a single new one. The clan still holds together. The House of Gilbey is a family business still, welded and maintained by long-tried trust and consanguinity. There lies its strength, its charm, its future.

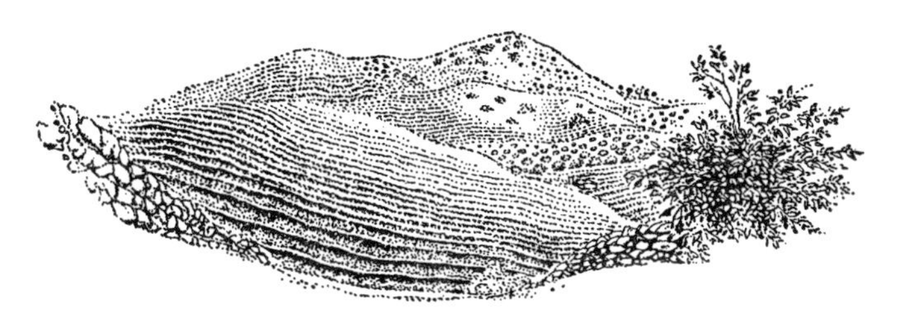

Index

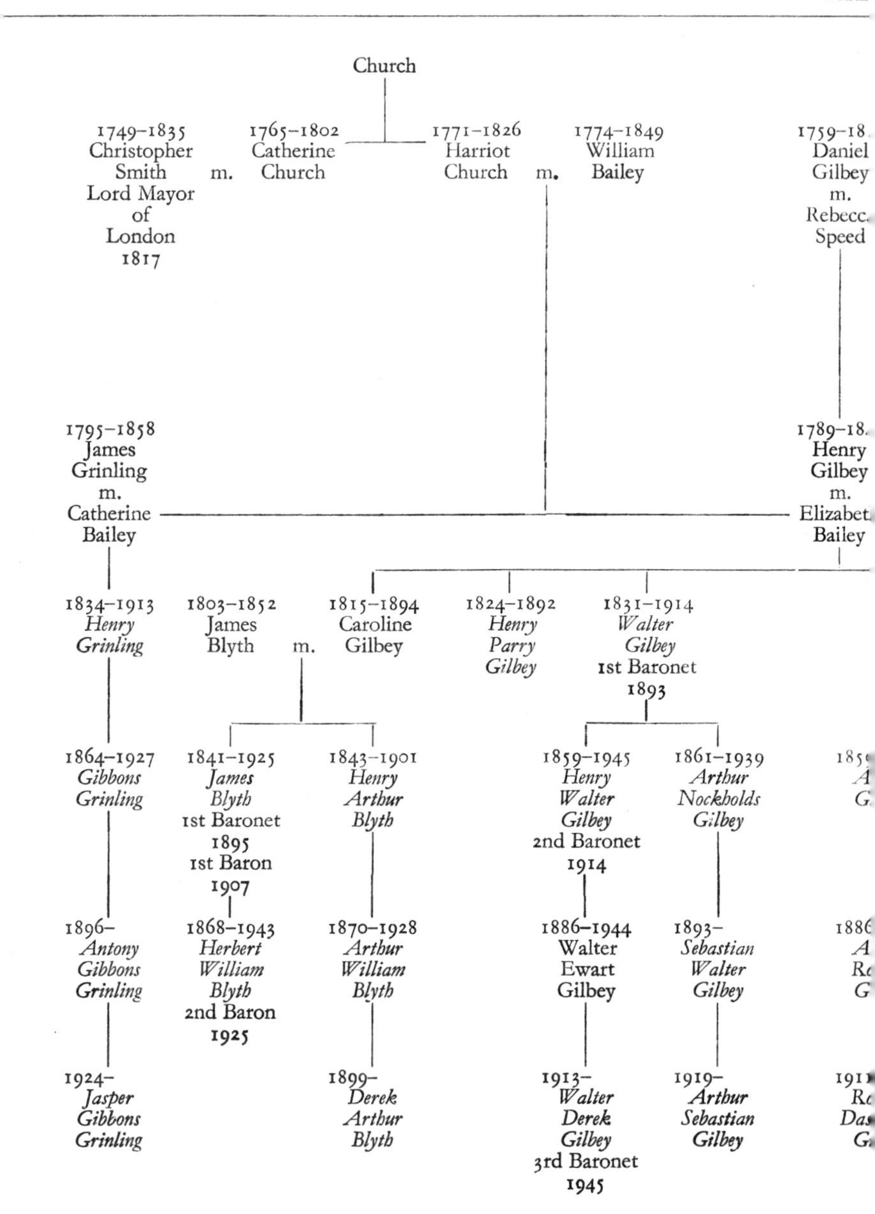
Church
1749–1835 Christopher Smith Lord Mayor of London 1817
m.
1765–1802 Catherine Church
1771–1826 Harriot Church
m.
1774–1849 William Bailey
1759–18 Daniel Gilbey m. Rebecc Speed
1795–1858 James Grinling m. Catherine Bailey
1789–18 Henry Gilbey m. Elizabet Bailey
1834–1913 Henry Grinling
1803–1852 James Blyth
m.
1815–1894 Caroline Gilbey
1824–1892 Henry Parry Gilbey
1831–1914 Walter Gilbey 1st Baronet 1893
1864–1927 Gibbons Grinling
1841–1925 James Blyth 1st Baronet 1895 1st Baron 1907
1843–1901 Henry Arthur Blyth
1859–1945 Henry Walter Gilbey 2nd Baronet 1914
1861–1939 Arthur Nockholds Gilbey
1896– Antony Gibbons Grinling
1868–1943 Herbert William Blyth 2nd Baron 1925
1870–1928 Arthur William Blyth
1886–1944 Walter Ewart Gilbey
1893– Sebastian Walter Gilbey
1924– Jasper Gibbons Grinling
1899– Derek Arthur Blyth
1913– Walter Derek Gilbey 3rd Baronet 1945
1919– Arthur Sebastian Gilbey

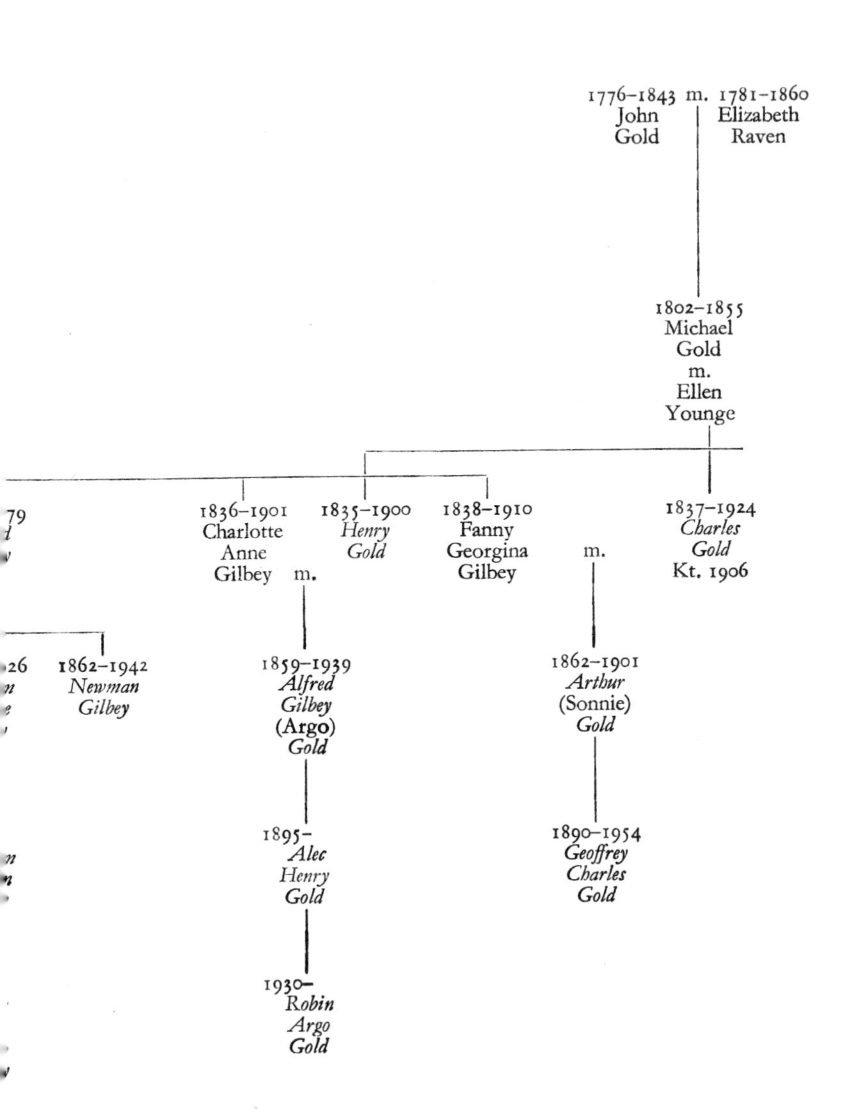
1776–1843 John Gold m. 1781–1860 Elizabeth Raven
1802–1855 Michael Gold m. Ellen Younge
79
1836–1901 Charlotte Anne Gilbey m.
1835–1900 Henry Gold
1838–1910 Fanny Georgina Gilbey
m.
1837–1924 Charles Gold Kt. 1906
26
1862–1942 Newman Gilbey
1859–1939 Alfred Gilbey (Argo) Gold
1862–1901 Arthur (Sonnie) Gold
1895– Alec Henry Gold
1890–1954 Geoffrey Charles Gold
1930– Robin Argo Gold